Praise for ~ *God Is in the Details*

"A must read! It reveals details of everyday life that may seem like chance or coincidence to some—but this shows us that sometimes the smallest details are meant to create the biggest impact."
—Lina Juncaj

"These stories awakened my heart to the reality that God is always present. It helped me to remember to stay open to the many ways source is looking to encourage, support, inspire, and challenge me."
—Dr. Tim Hogan

"Whether you're religious or not, you will find true knowledge in the book. It will enlighten one's perspective on looking on the bright side of situations. Eye Opening!"
—Toni McElreath

"*God Is in the Details* is my new mantra! The book reminds us that even when the worst things possible happen, love, light and blessings are right there for you. A WONDERFUL book about life!"
—J. Lane

God
is in
the
Details

ALSO BY CATHERINE WILCOX

Sacred Series Books

· Guides for Conscious Change ·

Sacred Grief

Sacred Prosperity

Sacred Space

Sacred Relationship

God is in the Details

Little stories to nourish your faith

Catherine Wilcox

Cudjoe Key, Florida

Published by Northstar Manuals, LLC
701 Spanish Main Dr., #215
Cudjoe Key, FL 33042
586-469-0840
Visit our Web Site at www.northstarmanuals.com
Email us at information@northstarmanuals.com

ISBN 978-1-953860-69-9

Table of Contents

Preface

There is a productive manifestation power that dwells within all of us. What is it? It's the potential to experience a grace-filled life. We all have this manifestation power, but few of us recognize it, and more importantly, employ it. This force is innate and available to all regardless of the magnitude of the need. For example, on a Monday in a restaurant, I tasted some delicious onion soup and created a mental intention that I would like to find a recipe for onion soup. On the following Wednesday, I had a series of business appointments scheduled. I normally grab something from my four-foot-high reading pile to read in between my meetings.

Serendipitously, I grabbed a vegetarian magazine that I had never even opened from almost the bottom of the pile. It was three months old.

I never did get a chance to glance at that magazine on Wednesday, but on Thursday it was sitting on my desk ready to return to the reading pile. While on hold during a phone call, I casually opened the magazine encouraged by the fact that I never like to return something to that pile once it makes its way out. I open up right to the page that contained a French onion soup recipe. How does that happen?

A better understanding of Divine guidance is the subject of this book—to help us learn to understand that our life paths are divinely designed right down to the minutest details. The more we recognize the hand of God in every aspect of our human existence and acknowledge and appreciate it, the closer we, as individuals and ultimately collectively, will be able to dance in happiness no matter the circumstances we are encountering at the moment.

The idea for this book came after my husband suddenly died while on a Caribbean cruise. When I started to finally write, I began writing four books at one time. Some of the research I did for one book ended up in a different book. I began to organize my research so I could easily find it. Oftentimes, I'd enter my writing studio with a specific mission on my mind. I would start that mission and in a matter of minutes be directed to an altogether different plan for that day, changing the course of that day's writing activity.

We are always being reminded, consciously and subliminally, that there is a power greater than ourselves directing the flow of our lives. I call these God's details. This book is about helping you to see God in every detail. Recurring animal sightings (totems), dreams, and seemingly coincidental events are just a few of the ways we experience God's details on a most regular basis.

One of the first times I came in contact with the idea of there being a bigger picture than what seems to meet the eye, or God being in all the details, was when my brand new Corvette was stolen thirty years before my writing journey began. The bottom line of the event was that shortly after it was stolen, I ended up in the hospital with pneumonia. My life at that time was a financial disaster, meaning I was without funds to pay any bills. Adding a hospital stay and the long recovery time needed for pneumonia to my current inventory of problems could have surely meant financial calamity.

In the end, the insurance company paid me almost the exact price that I originally paid for the car five years earlier. After paying the small loan balance off, I was able to pay all my bills with money left over while I recovered from pneumonia. It was then that I began to fully understand that there is always a force—I choose to call it God—that works to keep our lives whole and on its life path, whether we acknowledge it or not. The Bible verse, "What man means for evil, God means for good" (Genesis 50:20) began to come alive for me. A stolen car—evil. Money from it to pay bills—good.

This book was designed to plant seeds in your subconscious mind that every life event or occurrence is based in goodness. Further, that we live in a stream of potential energy where everything is always moving in the direction of the underlying orderliness of the universe. Orderliness is produced by God as His details.

The true stories in this book are perfect examples of the collective Soul's power in seeing to "God's will be done." These collections of modern day parables clearly show that the amazing power of the "collective" mind is much greater than an individual's ability to do for itself. In other words, God is still in the business of miracle making even if it doesn't look as amazing as Jesus turning wine into water or feeding 5,000 people with two fish and five loaves of bread.

You will see yourself somewhere in this book and when you do, transform what may still resonate as a hurtful or sad time into a learned, soulful lesson. It's never too late to take a circumstance that appears dark and use it to channel more light into your life. Nothing is impossible if we will only remember that God IS in every detail of our life.

God IS in every detail whether you ascribe to this truth or not. When we have a better understanding of this and how it relates to our daily living we can begin to experience less of the sadness that comes with grief, loss, disabilities, loneliness, etc.

It is the collective Soul that prods the spirit self through modern day miracles seeking to aid in transcending our minds away from faithlessness and useless emotions. God's details are intended to give us light-filled experiences at every turn and, further, to prepare us for a light-filled future so that we can spread love to the four corners of this planet. Period.

While I have collected God detail stories over the years, a lot of the stories here happened to me. Those I have collected from others may have name changes. This also will explain the different voices the stories are written in. Everyone is true without embellishment. My hope in writing this book is that we will all come to better recognize the Divine guidance in our lives and in so doing, see all the events in our lives as God's way of "knitting" the collective into the realization of the "one heart" mindedness.

The new millennium has opened a portal of change to our planet. This new portal is a God detail on a large scale intended to open us all up to channel more compassion, joy, and peace not only for our individual lives but also to everyone we meet, and they meet, and they meet, and they meet. And so it is.

Chapter 1

Simple Details

My first noticeable connection to God in all of my details was when I was on my way to the hospital in 1979. I was in the bathtub soaking when I received a phone call indicating that my three-year-old daughter was hurt and I needed to get to St. John's Hospital immediately. She was with her father for a weekend visitation outing.

I lived on a service drive of a new expressway that just opened two days before the fateful call. I was at the hospital in twelve minutes. I still marvel at this timing detail as prior to this new expressway, the same trip on surface roads would have been at least fifty minutes. Even though no one told me on the phone, I innately knew that my daughter had died and I needed to be at the hospital as quickly as possible. Tears streamed from my eyes the entire ride. I remember thanking God for parting the cars like the Red Sea as I drove.

When you are in the midst of the simple details of Master Soul at work, be sure to express gratitude. This can be very challenging. Life's circumstances happen. Receiving grace to move through them is a God detail. Gratitude is also a very important ingredient to the propagation of receiving more grace.

See if you can identify with some of the simple details others have experienced in the stories told throughout this book.

Street Guidance

Lindsay tells us her story:

Months after my husband died, I met Glen. I was not ready for a new relationship and told Glen so. He promised me he would be very respectful of my feelings, and true to his word. He was very slow and gentle in his pursuit of my friendship.

Two months into our very slow dating process, I traveled out of town alone to Petoskey, Michigan on business. Halloween was coming. My late husband and I spent every Halloween with our friends, Ron and Jan, for the last eight years, donning zany costumes and rustling up a little trouble to enjoy ourselves. I must admit all the while driving, I was grieving over the disappointment of not having my husband to "dress up and play with."

While driving I pondered what new plans I would be making for Halloween that year. Jan called and invited me (and one other person I wanted) to join them on a Halloween road rally where costumes were mandatory. I told her I wasn't sure about asking Glen. Internally, I wasn't sure about bringing a new man into my husband's territory. That is a major step in the grief process. We discussed a theme for our car and decided upon the Wizard of Oz, as I had every costume except the Tin Man in my costume collection.

Petoskey, Michigan is a beautiful place to shop, so after my business was complete, I went into town to see what I could find when I came upon the *Halloween Book of Costumes*. I opened it up to scan it and on the page I opened it to, were directions on how to create a Tin Man outfit. While watching for the receipt to print out, I noticed the address of the store was on Glen Street. I knew then that it was time to take the next step and let Glen more deeply into my life. I called him to see if he was interested in attending a Halloween party as the Tin Man. He had never attended a Halloween party in his life! Tall and lanky, he made a great Tin Man.

Q & A

One of the many God details I recognized came during the grieving process after my husband's death. Afterwards, certain questions continued to loom in my mind. You know, the usual. Did I let him know how much I loved him? Is Bill safe and loved where he is? Will I ever be able to love like that again? Will there ever be any other sweet, single men to love? Amazingly with each question, I was provided an answer.

The first was, did I ever let Billy know how much I loved him. Several days after the memorial service, as I started to clean out his desk and closet, I found at least fifteen greeting cards I had sent him (he was a pack rat) from as long as fifteen years earlier to as recent as the previous Easter. They were all filled with loving thoughts and messages from me that he had held on to and I had long forgotten about.

Then, three weeks to the day of his passing, I was on my way to the beauty salon crying my eyes out thinking, "Billy, I hope you're safe and in heaven." When I looked up, I noticed that on the license plate ahead of me were the letters R E E N I E. Amazingly, that was Bill's mother's name, the name and the spelling of it most uncommon. In real time my question was answered. I knew not to worry any longer.

Four weeks to the day of Bill's passing another question was clearly eliminated. It is normal when grieving to wonder where your life is going because loss creates holes both in our hearts and our routines. I enjoyed being married to Bill and had wondered if I would ever find a kind, sweet man to share the rest of my life with. That day, I had three different appointments with three different prospects to show property. Somehow in our conversations, all three managed to inform me they were single men. They appeared kind and considerate. I had my wedding rings on, so they didn't know I was a widow, but God was answering one more of my concerns in God detail fashion.

When's the last time you were looking for answers? It's common for the mind to wonder about things. Are you listening? God provides. Be on the lookout. God's details take on many forms.

A Father's Love

In 1975, Al was twenty-four when his parents divorced. His father, Richard, had left his mother for another woman.

As soon as the divorce was final, Richard married Phyllis, who had an emotionally troubled son. William was twelve years old. Al's father moved out of state and basically lost contact with Al because of all the familial emotions that occur with divorce. Al's dad took on the raising of Phyllis's son as his own. Even at twenty-four years of age, Al was emotionally traumatized by the disconnect he felt from the loss of his father. Al felt replaced by Richard's son, William.

It was twenty years later that Al saw the hand of God in his father's story. After settling in, Richard immediately enrolled William into an all-boys school in Sebastian, Florida hoping to help William find some peace. He then also legally adopted him as his own. It took some years for William to smooth out his emotional issues. He stayed at the facility and eventually, twenty-two years later, became the director of the boys school that helped him change his life.

Al tells this story because in the big picture, he saw that his father's mission was clearly about guiding William to a place where he could ultimately make a difference in the lives of thousands of other young boys. Al retired, selling a very lucrative printing business and dedicated a good portion of those proceeds to—you guessed it!—the center in Florida for troubled boys. From angry to grateful. That switch in emotions is significant in itself. Seeing that William was led to a path of change to help others continued by his father, helped Al see that what looked like a mess actually had a purpose on many levels.

A Purpose-Filled Delay

Sharon, a successful Real Estate Broker from Maryland, decided to sell her house and move to Key West. After her house sold, she signed up for a class at the Hyatt in Key West in an effort to obtain employment there. The course was required to get into their employment system and only given twice a year. Her closing was scheduled one week before the class started.

Sharon was really upset when the closing on her home in Maryland was delayed for a week causing her to miss the Hyatt class. However, upon her arrival in Key West, she immediately found an employment ad for an upscale jewelry store that she had loved shopping at during her many, many vacation visits to the Florida Keys. Sharon later learned that they only ran that ad for one day.

Now, three years later, Sharon is still selling jewelry, making a very good living, and more importantly doing something she really, really loves. She is still grateful to this day that the closing on her home was delayed. All delays have God at their center.

Next time you're delayed, try looking for the God detail in the delay. We will never know about the car accident we missed or the product that was faulty and sold out before we made it to the store. But you can be sure that delays have a purpose. Accept them and be grateful rather than frustrated or angry when delays occur.

There's always a reason. Just ask those people who were delayed on September 11, 2001, from getting to work at the Trade Center in New York City.

A Christmas Gift

We were having new granite installed in our kitchen just in time for the Christmas holidays. In fact, I was playing Celine Dion's Christmas album while the granite was being installed. In one area, the granite overhang was so large that the installers said they would have to go back to the shop and build two supports under it at an additional cost. I asked them if there was any other way to do it because the supports would be unsightly and in the way of people sitting at the counter. Their reply was an emphatic NO!

Resigned to this, I went about my household chores. One of the installers casually mentioned how much his wife liked Celine Dion and what was the name of the album so he could get it for her.

Just the day before, I was going through my Christmas albums and noticed I had a duplicate CD of that very same Celine Dion album.

Having no need for two, I put the CD in a gift bag, gave it to the installer, and told him to give his wife her first gift of the season. He was grateful. So grateful, in fact, that when he came back the next day to finish installing, he had devised a way to put steel rods in the granite so that no supports were needed. They didn't charge me (a usual $500 charge) either.

I never noticed the two Dion albums before and had no idea how both even landed in my collection. I do know, however, that the CD gift was the reason the granite was installed without those ugly supports. I have fifteen Christmas CDs. Why did I select the Dion one? I often still tingle every time I sit at the kitchen counter and feel those steel rods embedded in the granite as a most fabulous reminder of the simplicity of God's details.

A Scholarship

Wheldon was born in Texas where his family lived in tents to survive as his father was a migrant farm hand. This family, seeking a better life, moved to Oklahoma when he was five, just in time for the big dust storms that left Oklahoma barren. Shortly thereafter, they moved to California where his family, which by now totaled nine, spent five years driving up and down the California coast working as farm hands.

Consequently, Wheldon attended eleven different elementary schools, which represented the only stability he knew.

As a result of WWII, his father was able to secure a job in a naval boatyard, and the family was finally able to settle in a small California town. When Wheldon was fourteen, he met his future bride who lived in even a smaller town eight miles west. Through a series of events, two years later, Dee and Wheldon became inseparable. Dee was only fifteen-years-old.

As a senior in high school, Wheldon's desire was to go to college. He was strongly encouraged by several of his teachers, but funds were unavailable.

Meanwhile, eight miles away, Dee was working in her high school as a secretary when she opened a letter that was offering a scholarship to the local university "teacher's college." Wheldon filled out the application after much prodding from Dee. He used old, yellowing, torn paper and pencil, as it was all he could afford, to write his request for the scholarship. Much to his surprise, he was accepted and received the $300, four-year scholarship that allowed him to enroll at the university. Fortunately, one of his neighbors was connected to the owner of a boarding house near the college. Wheldon paid for his room and board as a cook in that boarding house until Dee and Wheldon married during his sophomore year.

With Dee working and paying rent, Wheldon graduated and started teaching fifth grade science. He was recruited in his first year of teaching by a local county to head the "startup" of a Museum of Science largely made up of live animals used to teach children about nature. It was during his four-year stint at the museum that he earned his master's degree.

While at university working on his master's degree, the science department asked if he could fill in as a teacher for three weeks to cover for someone who took ill. The rest is history!

Wheldon went on to get his Doctorate in Natural Sciences, and for twenty-four years taught at the same university he received that scholarship to as Professor of Natural Science where his job was to train teachers how to teach science.

At his funeral celebration, the theme was, "One person who taught millions." Every conversation you would have with Wheldon would cause you to walk away with a new idea or new piece of information to treasure.

Wheldon passed at eighty-seven years young. From living in tents, and eleven different elementary schools, to Professor of Natural Science at a prestigious college. Only God could have been in charge of that small detail where Dee opened the mail to reveal the offer of a scholarship that ultimately lead Wheldon on his life path of "one person who taught millions."

Want Ads

After finding a tenant for their house, Betty, forty-five years old, her husband, Paul, fifty years old, and their seven-year-old daughter, Monica, moved out of their home state to Utah. They took what fit in their minivan, and stored the rest of their belongings. Betty sold her publishing company five years earlier and had lived off the proceeds. Paul had just sold off a house he had built for resale and barely broke even. They took $6,000 with them.

After setting up house in a 900 square foot apartment (the home they left behind was 4,000 square feet) they both began to look for jobs. Their purpose in moving was to get out of the business-world rat race and find something they loved doing rather than working for the money. Paul, a ski instructor as a college student, returned to the hills and instantly found work as a ski instructor, so he was happy. For Betty, the challenge was a little more difficult. She was trained in the publishing business, and there was no market for that in their new town, not to mention that she had promised herself she would never return to publishing when she sold her business. She wanted stress-free employment only!

Three weeks after Paul started work, Betty had still not found employment, their money was almost gone, and now the pressure was on! Additionally, the house they left behind required a mortgage payment supplement from them of $900 a month to cover the difference in the rent they were receiving and the mortgage cost.

Betty found a want ad seeking a "troubled teen" counselor. The job entailed camping outside, eight days on, eight days off, foraging for food and dealing with six to eight troubled teens whose parents sent them to this "boot camp" because they were out of control and in need of a life change. The teens live in the wilderness for thirty days earning items like matches, food, fire, clothing, etc., to make their survival easier.

Although it had an appeal to Betty, (she had spent four years in the army) it would mean leaving Paul and Monica for sixteen days a month. The guilt was looming, and Betty thought about it and decided she shouldn't be leaving her family, even though she knew intuitively this could be the perfect opportunity she was looking for to fulfill her desires and the family coffers.

Two days later, Paul had brought the same newspaper home with the same ad circled and left it on the kitchen table for Betty to see. She explained to Paul that she had checked this job out, and gave him the details. He told her to go for it. Still unconvinced, two days after Paul left the ad on the table, Betty received a phone call from her sister in Ohio telling her that she had just sent her daughter, Betty's niece, to boot camp in Utah for sixty days because she had been in trouble again. It was the exact place that Betty had considered working.

Betty now knew that this was the job that was right for her at this time in her life. She took the job and had many wonderful personal experiences in the wilderness that she needed for the next stage of her life. More importantly, because Betty was gone eight days at a time, it gave father and daughter a chance to bond, which was something that never had a chance to bloom between them.

God's details often come at us from many difficult angles to help us formulate decisions. A song on the radio. A billboard with one igniting word. Are you listening?

Trickle Down Details

As an inducement to learning the books of the New Testament, I offered five dollars to the student in my Sunday school class who could recite the books in order on the following Sunday.

Much to my amazement, nine out of twenty-five preteens came prepared to win the five dollars. Since I had only one five dollar bill on me, I had to have them pick numbers to establish their reciting order. Then whoever succeeded first won the money.

David, a quiet kid, drew number one. Immediately, I felt a lot of negative energy in the room as the other eight prepared students were sending off resentful, jealous, and even angry thoughts at David that he would possibly win, eliminating their chance of winning.

Never wanting to miss an opportunity to reset young minds, I stopped dead in my tracks and asked the kids, "Who is upset that they didn't pick the number one?" Kids that age are so honest. Four of them raised their hands. They admitted to a variety of selfish, negative feelings toward David.

Curiously, I asked them if they would all like to win the five dollars. They naturally admitted they would. I told them that one of the laws of the universe is that we must want for others what we want for ourselves, and suggested that rather than expressing or feeling any of those negative energies about David that they instead pray that he accomplishes his goal to win the five dollars. Reminding them that there was great power in wanting for others what we want for ourselves, I asked them if they wanted to get some of that power too. When they all concurred, we collectively said a prayer together that David would easily and perfectly recite all of the books of the New Testament in order. The energy in the room changed immediately.

By now I'm sure you guessed that David recited those books in perfect order and with the greatest of ease. God was certainly in the details by allowing David to pick the number one. We proceeded to all other eight kids, and not one of them actually got past reciting the first seven books out of twenty-seven. But the details didn't stop there!

The following Sunday one of my students, Jack, came running into the room full of excitement to share his good news. In the last week, he was in a spelling bee between five local schools. It was down to the final two spellers, and Jack was one of them. He told us before the other contestant received her word in the final round, he silently said a prayer that she would spell it correctly. She didn't. He spelled his and the rest, as they say, is history.

A beautiful lifelong lesson learned by all because God took care of one detail: letting David, most likely the best prepared, be the first reciter of the New Testament books. Twenty-five young sponge minds received first-hand experience not only of the power of collective prayer, but also in the results of success when you remove a personalized and self-centered agenda from the equation.

One simple detail designed and produced by the Divine offers a new way of living to a classroom of children in the prime of their learning. God's amazing timing. Do you recall any details like this from your younger years?

Small Still Voices

We all know someone who seems to have the universe continuously responding to their every need. This is not magic or good fortune. Most likely it is someone who has learned to tap into the complete database of answers via their Soul connection. No one person is more qualified or entitled to the receipt of this Soul connection over anyone else. Some people are more intuitive because they have learned how to "plug-in" to Creator Source using various methods—living in now moments, meditation, prayer, noticing signs, recognizing their dreams, etc.

I had been selling real estate for eight years when I showed a vacant house to a very large man. The lockbox containing the key to unlock the door was on the door around the corner to the rear of the house. Halfway up the driveway, a strong wave of fear came over me. I immediately stopped and informed this prospective buyer that I was unable to show him the house as I sensed danger. I would have to call someone to accompany us. He reached inside his jacket and pulled out a sheriff's badge. He was carrying a gun. I had sensed it. That was my small, still voice advising me.

Although it is believed that women naturally have a deeper connection with intuitive energy, anyone can make a choice to turn to passive (not aggressive) energy for their solution when in the midst of any challenge. Passivity, in most situations, often allows us to hear that small, still voice. When you listen to it and honor it at all times, regardless of how crazy or off-base it may seem, the small still voice authored by God will offer up this Divine guidance in even the most mundane of events.

Listening up and taking action in accordance with what you hear and feel can reinforce to the Soul, which is the connector of the little voice to your mind, that you are willing to experience and utilize a plan other than your own human willfulness.

See if you resonate with some of the following parables.

Suicide Counselor

My life career before writing was commercial real estate brokering. One event that I clearly remember was when I had scheduled a closing for a vacant piece of commercial property for December 15. Two days before the closing, I received word from the title company that they discovered an anomaly in the chain of title that needed researching. I should have been told of this issue much earlier, but Tammy, the processor/closer, had been on vacation and no one was handling her files while she was gone.

In my forty-some years in the business, I had never seen a title problem like this. I sold the property to a college fifteen years earlier, and the title was good then. Nonetheless, we canceled the closing. Three days later after the title company apologized for the error, we scheduled the closing for December 23. Closing documents were sent to all parties including respective legal counsels.

I called the purchaser on December 22, the day before the scheduled closing, to confirm closing for the next day only to be told that his attorney had never received the documents. He couldn't close without attorney review, but said he could close on the twenty-sixth of the month. However, in checking with the seller, she would be out of town until January 4. I scheduled the closing for January 5 at 1:00 p.m. and held my breath hoping all parties were available to close.

I happened to be out of town the week of the closing, so I informed the closer at the title company the day before the closing that if there were any problems, I would be available to resolve them so please call or email me.

As it worked out on the fifth, a group of us went to an afternoon movie matinee which started at 12:15 p.m. Naturally, I had to shut my phone ringer off and didn't think another thing about the closing. However, I received an "urge" to check my emails during the movie, and sure enough, I saw an email from the closer that said there was a problem with the buyer's bank concerning the wire transfer of funds to close with. I scurried out of the theatre to resolve this. Before I was able to call the title company, I saw (remember the ringer is off) a call coming in from Phyllis, one of my employees that I have a mother-daughter relationship with. I answered her call only to hear Phyllis' hysterical voice on the other line explaining that she went home unexpectedly for lunch to find her twenty-year-old daughter ready to execute plans for suicide. After fifteen minutes on the phone, I calmed Phyllis down and walked her through what she could do to help her daughter in crisis. I listened to her and offered advice both for her and her daughter. She thanked me a hundred times for my help.

I then called the closer after this call and began asking questions about the email she sent. After listening patiently to me, she said, "You didn't see my second email did you?" After I replied, "No," she said, "The buyer called the bank and the funds to close arrived." Relieved, I walked back into the theatre to finish the show.

As soon as I sat down, I was overwhelmed with awe. In fact, I had a hard time focusing on the movie. Had I not received the urge, a God detail, to check my emails during the movie, I would have never responded to Phyllis' call as my phone's ringer was turned off. I was even more amazed as I thought about all the crazy and unusual circumstances that caused a simple closing that was originally scheduled for December 15 to be delayed by a series of circumstances to a date and exact time when I would be able to answer Phyllis' harried call and be of service to her.

Taken aback by all of this, the next day I felt another "urge" to share this with Tammy from the title company whom I had many nice conversations with during the three months before the closing. The next day, January 6, I texted Tammy telling her that if it wasn't for her emailing me when she did and me getting some type of mental telepathic message from her to look at my emails, I would not have been able to help an employee deal with a suicidal daughter.

About two hours later I received a call from Tammy. She sounded teary-eyed as she revealed to me that January 6 marked the three-year anniversary of the suicide of her nineteen-year-old son. She related that she felt so happy that "God used her" to help prevent another parent from having to go through the loss and sadness of losing a child. Even more amazing to me was that I lost a child to an automobile accident on January 6, forty-five years earlier. We talked for about an hour where I shared with her my recovery process after losing my daughter.

This is an amazing display of God connecting the dots from an experience of forty-five years ago between many different entities (Title Company, bank wires, a seller, a closer, and me) to help bring peace to the mother of a victim of suicide and to help a mother of a possible suicide. God used me as a conduit in a highly detailed fashion.

Small still voices create powerful urges. They are designed to protect us, help us protect others and bring light to the collective. Artists, writers, musicians, politicians, truck drivers, moms, and dads—everyone receives them. Listening to them and taking action in accordance with them is our job and certainly God's good pleasure to provide. Take action when guided, and you will find the still small voice will beam louder and more often for you.

Oh, did I mention the movie was called "The Greatest Show on Earth"? Indeed!

Release

Cheryl, who was widowed from a chiropractor five years earlier, decided to surrender some antique collectibles of his that she was clinging to that contained many memories of her late husband. She had been remarried for several years when she felt that the time was right to let both the items and memories go.

These antique "collectibles" consisted of four 33 1/3 rpm records that were lectures of holistic healing recorded in the late 1950s, a gizmo from that era that measured body heat, and a book written in the 1980s entitled *Applied Kinesiology.*

Never a person to waste anything, Cheryl felt an urging to gift them to her new chiropractor, who was in his mid-sixties and ironically had worked with the man who co-authored the *Applied Kinesiology* book.

One Tuesday afternoon at an appointment with the chiropractor scheduled three weeks earlier, Cheryl brought in the bag of goodies. The chiropractor grabbed the book and, after hugging her with glee, told her the following tale:

He had taught a seminar the previous weekend. In preparation for the seminar, he had looked everywhere for his copy of *Applied Kinesiology* to no avail. It just so happened on that same day, two hours before Cheryl's appointment, the widow of the author of the book also had an appointment with him. He asked the widow if she had any copies of the book laying around. She did not.

His joy and excitement at receiving Cheryl's husband's book filled the entire office.

Are you listening to those small still voice messages regarding the things it's time for you to release?

The Perfect Storm

Hugh owned a beautiful three-acre parcel of land on Lake St. Clair for twenty years. It was one of the few really stunning pieces of land left in the small waterfront community. Originally owned by a total of four partners, over the years Hugh bought his other three partners out to become the sole owner. At seventy-seven years young, he really wasn't sure why he held it for so long and felt like he was past his prime to begin any building projects.

Hugh always attended a local lumber yard's annual reward-for-contractors junket. This year he met Jeff, a thirty-eight-year-old owner of a building company at the junket.

Dino, a fifty-eight-year-old residential builder, was also attending this year's four-day junket to Aruba where he met Jeff. Sitting together on a plane on the way home afforded the three of them an opportunity to become better acquainted. They exchanged cards before deplaning.

About three weeks later, Dino was driving from an appointment and got the idea, or guidance rather, to stop in and visit Jeff since he was in the neighborhood as he wanted to see what kind of operation Jeff had.

At the same time, Hugh just happened to have stopped by to visit Jeff. The three clicked immediately, and a beautiful building partnership was born between the three of them, and a new subdivision was built by this trio partnership.

There certainly are no accidents. Are you listening to your Divine guidance? Your small voice?

Inner Guidance

Eighteen months after her husband Hank died, Dorothy was shopping one Saturday when a voice in her head said, "You'd better hurry, or you'll miss the 6:30 p.m. mass at church." She had stopped going to church a year earlier because she was unable to stop crying while she was there. After six months of the uncontrollable sobbing during Saturday night services, she just gave up going.

Still shopping at 5:30 p.m., that same voice urged her to leave the store to get to church. After telling the voice in her head she was not planning on going to church, she moved on to another store as if to let that nagging voice know she was firm in her decision. The third time she heard that nagging voice, she was in her car on the way home. Dorothy started laughing at the nagging inner voice, vehemently stating that she had things to do at home when she noticed that her car had just passed the street she needed to turn on to pull into her driveway. Before she knew it, Dorothy was in her church parking lot. She had succumbed to the nagging voice and was even on time for the

6:30 p.m. service. Imagine her amazement when the priest announced in his welcoming remarks that this was a "special" mass for those people who needed healing on a physical, emotional, and spiritual level over the loss of a loved one. The message was exactly what Dorothy needed to hear to move on with her life.

Chapter 2

Healing Details

FRESHLY MARRIED SOME SEVEN MONTHS EARLIER, WE RETURNED HOME from a weirdly abnormal vacation to find waiting in our mail pile a sealed letter from Kris, my husband's forty-five-year-old daughter. The reason for our "depressing" get-away was confirmed in that four-page handwritten letter which, after reading it, my husband handed to me and declared, "Here, this is your problem."

Kris, who was still weary from her father leaving her mother and sister thirty-four years earlier for another woman, was lambasting me for being her father's choice for his bride in that letter. I only read the first accusatory paragraph before ripping it to shreds while suggesting to my husband that I wanted a divorce, as I was unwilling to take on the angst from his daughters that belonged to someone else, especially without his support.

To avoid divorce, we attended counseling for about six months before my husband was ready to bring in his daughters at the request of the counselor.

Interestingly enough, my own mother's father left her mother for another woman when my mother was Kris's age. Although never spoken about with my mother, our relationship was infused with the chronic pain of the loss of my mother's father through divorce which was an exact replica of the issue Kris was having with her father. For that reason, I saw this as a Soul guiding experience. I was not angry, did not withhold sex, and fully supported the big picture, that is, familial healing even though I was forbidden to attend family functions. This meant my husband was banned as well. Through counseling, he came to understand his past role as the "star" of the familial battle we were in.

Through all of this, the only thing I was personally interested in was an apology from my husband for initially "blaming" me for this situation.

It was almost eleven months later, and I had not received any conciliatory response in any form from my husband. In many of the details of my daily spiritual reading practice, everything that landed in my day to read was fully focused on staying in the light no matter what was going on around me. I could not have moved forward into the light without those reading materials that simply appeared for me during those eleven months.

Then one day it struck me. The law of prosperity states that if you want something, you must first give it away. It dawned on me that I must write my husband a letter of forgiveness for my heart to heal. This thought came on a Saturday as I was home alone working in the garden. I stopped to find some writing paper and a pen.

Prior to our marriage, I had written a lot of "love" letters to my husband that I never mailed to him. Instead, as a wedding gift, I put the notes in a beautiful, artsy box. We still select one now and then, ten years later, and read it. The letter I was about to write was secretly going in this box to be found by him someday in God's timing.

So I wrote and wrote and wrote, giant tears streaming from my heart through tiny little tear ducts. Deposited in the box, I resumed my garden work feeling free. It no longer mattered if my husband ever apologized to me or not.

Later that day, after checking the US mailbox, my elated emotions were quickly reversed when in the mail came another sealed envelope from Kris. I was convinced that it was more of the same as the original letter as I had not seen or talked to his two daughters in over a year. However, the five-year-old daughter of Kris, our granddaughter, had spent the night with us on several occasions. My husband came home several hours after I saw the mail. I did not open it and was unable to control my interior seething.

This time it was me who tossed the letter at my husband and stammered that I was done with this game and his family. I had finally burst at the seams from all of the emotion that this whole debacle had multiplied in me from my childhood to this point. He sequestered himself away from me to read the letter.

Ten minutes later he found me in the garden still angry as a hornet and tossed me the newly received letter. The tears were uncontrollable! Inside that envelope was a drawing of a little girl (our five-year-old granddaughter) standing in the middle of two stick figures of the opposite sex holding that little girl's hands. There was the sun and flowers and hearts drawn everywhere. Although a great God detail and one would think a fabulous ending to a year of familial strife, there was still more.

My husband handed me a beautiful handwritten note he had written that day while alone, apologizing to me for putting me through the "daughter" thing. He thanked me for my strength and honored my character in his eyes and the eyes of God. When he handed me the letter, he said he was waiting for the perfect time to give it to me and knew when our granddaughter's drawing stirred up the past it was the perfect time.

Looking back on this timely event in all of our lives, one can see God was at the center of all the details from my need to heal over my mother's pain of loss from her father, to the need of my daughters-in-law who still harbored their various issues over their own parent's divorce.

I truly believe that daughter number two, forty-two years old and never married, benefitted the most from the whole event. She had a propensity to attract creepy men which can be a byproduct of the childhood wounding of a divorce. Through the counseling they all shared, I believe healing started for her. Several years later a wonderful man found her, and she finally entered the ultimate relationship dance we call marriage.

God's details are nothing short of miracles at work daily in our lives. Acknowledgment of the wonders that constantly surround us is necessary to experience these miracles continually.

At any given moment, we are living in either light or darkness, depending on our choices. Thankfully the decision is always ours. God's details/miracles are always at work in our lives every moment of every day. Rejoice and be glad in them!

MS

Heather was diagnosed in 2000, at age thirty-two, with Multiple Sclerosis. Married to Bill, an electrical engineer at twenty-one, she earned a degree in Management Information Systems. By thirty-six, her physical condition deteriorated so badly that she was partially blind, paralyzed, and completely disoriented. The doctors told the family that

Heather would ultimately end up as "a slobbering idiot tied to a wheelchair."

Before that in 1988, Earl, Heather's father, had invested some money with a young Harvard graduate, John, who Earl met as a result of John cold calling for new customers. One year into the investment, Earl's capital had doubled. John called and suggested that Earl liquidate and invest in a company called Centocor, a pharmaceutical company. Earl broke his own unwritten investment rules and bought this stock on a significant margin.

Within months, Centocor, a subsidiary of Johnson & Johnson whose name was later changed to Janssen Biotech, Inc., was caught falsifying data and lying on their application. Because of this, the FDA would not approve their application for the miracle drug that had initially caused their stock to double—which is why Earl bought the stock in the first place. Instead, the lack of FDA approval caused the stock to tank. All of Earl's investment was lost. Even worse, Earl had to find $40,000 to cover his margin call due to the declining value of the stock compared to his purchase price.

In 1990, John's boss, Lars, moved to another brokerage house. Lars contacted Earl and complimented him on how quickly he responded to the margin call. He apologized for Earl's loss and offered to help Earl pick up the pieces of his investment portfolio.

Lars did just as he promised and eventually, Earl had more than recouped his losses with Lars's help. In this process they became friends. It was twelve years later that Heather was diagnosed with MS.

Earl was dealing with his daughter's devastating diagnoses when Lars happened to call about an investment opportunity. Upon hearing about Heather, Lars related to Earl that he had a client who also had had MS. Earl asked why he said he "had" MS as Earl was told there is no cure. Lars encouraged Earl to call his previous client, Joe, who no longer exhibited symptoms of the debilitating disease.

Earl called Joe and learned that Joe went to Monterey, New York for "Alternating Frequency Electro Magnetic Treatments." Joe told him that he went into the hospital a drooling idiot and walked out three weeks later carrying his wheelchair. He had been MS free for nine years when Earl found him.

The Monterey Clinic was no longer treating MS with Alternating Frequency Electro-Magnetic Treatments, but Joe knew the investor of the machine and sponsored a meeting between Earl, the investor, and Dr. Davidson, the inventor.

Dr. Davidson was retired but gave Earl access to the patents for his Electro-Magnetic Treatment Machine. In God's perfect detail, Heather's husband who was an electrical engineer and Earl, a retired engineer, built in Heather's basement the machine that ultimately brought Heather to a miraculous recovery including 20/20 vision, and the ability to walk entirely unaided. Heather now spends her days fully caring for her four children.

Twelve years earlier, the wheels were put into motion by God to offer a solution to one person's debilitating disease. Can you recognize the historical "wheels in motion" of your own life?

Health Designed Delay

Landing for my winter hiatus in Florida, I had to call my phone carrier to activate my Wi-Fi hotspot connection. It was a Sunday afternoon by the time I was unpacked and able to devote a few minutes of concentrated time to this project.

As I was dialing, my husband coerced me into committing to a five-mile bike ride to the post office. I had not taken much exercise in the past three days as I had been experiencing severe back pain, but being the usual energizer bunny that I am, agreed to go with him in spite of how I felt when my phone project was complete.

Typically it takes about fifteen minutes to activate my hotspot with the carrier. However, after thirty minutes on the phone, my husband lost his patience and left without me. I ended up being on the phone for 117 minutes (the last twenty minutes on hold with only music playing) before I hung up and called back and asked to speak to a supervisor.

I used everything I had to keep my composure after spending 117 minutes, missing a bike ride, and still not activating my hotspot while talking to the supervisor. My husband walked in from his ride just as my hot spot became activated.

Still in back pain and not feeling well, I walked into a doctor's office first thing Monday morning only to discover I had a severe kidney/urinary tract infection. Seeking medical instruction, I asked if it would be alright to resume some physical exercise that day. He looked at me like I was crazy. "Absolutely not!" was his emphatic reply. He said I needed to rest as these type of infections can move through the bloodstream quicker during exercise. He told me that even in this day and age, even in America, people die from organ infections such as I had.

So, in essence, the 117 minute, unproductive (or was it?) phone call was part of the master plan, God's details, to possibly prevent my untimely death. Of course, we will never know that for sure, and I'm glad I didn't have to find out. In my mind, I could clearly see the hand of God in this small episodic event—and grateful for it.

Are you able to understand delays and changes in your plans as a benefit rather than an annoyance? Become aware and then give thanks for those life interruptions. The more gratitude you can find over life's interruptions that may irk you, the better your connection to the life-giving solutions that are alive in God's details.

Young Artist

When asked, Garry Campbell, an artist from Jamaica who creates paintings of fruit and people, explained his path in becoming an artist.

When he was six years old, one of his neighbors, Jay, an artist, could no longer afford his rent and was being evicted. Garry's mom helped the neighbor move. To thank her and Garry, he gave Garry one of his paintings. Garry will tell you that for a good while he hated the artwork. He'd rather have had money for his time.

The painting hung in his bedroom for three years when, at nine years old, Garry sketched the painting on his own canvas. Several people commented on how Garry's sketch was better than the original. Several weeks later both pieces of art were stolen. Garry so missed the art he had come to enjoy that he had begun to paint in order to replace the wall hanging. An artist was born.

Is the message here to rethink what you hate? Perhaps it's to reach back and think about what early inspirations you ignored. Either way, healing any occurring negative emotions are inspired by God details that are always at play in our lives. You decide!

Chapter 3

Folks in Your Way

THERE IS A MOVIE CALLED *THE FOUR FEATHERS* ABOUT FOUR BRITISH soldiers who go off to a foreign desert country together to fight in battle. Somehow the main character, Harry, gets stranded and is left in the desert for dead. A big, burly native comes across him in the sand, rescues him, and promises to protect him. The rest of the movie is about this native, Abu, following Harry and saving his backside many times.

Near the end of the movie, after many harrowing rescues, it is time for Harry to say goodbye to Abu. Harry asks Abu during their farewell dialogue, why he protected him so much. Abu responded, "Because God put you in my way!"

There are no accidents! God, through the urging of our Soul, uses people to prod us along on our life path. Even bad intentioned people are used by God to urge growth and change for both you and them on individualized and collective levels. A wife-beating husband is used to teach a woman to stand tall in her truth. The horrific incident 9-11 sparked a needed global consciousness change.

At any rate, unless you are a hermit, folks are constantly in our way. Hopefully, these parables will cause you to examine and appreciate the folks that appear in your way and those in whose way you are. Often when we can see as blessings the folks in our way and actually see the positive effects they bring to us, light-filled experiences will not be far behind.

Running Angel

Nia, a thirty-year-old ex-regional VP for a health and wellness company, had been invited by some friends at her gym to run a ten-mile race. She had run 6.4 miles in the past, but was unsure about running a ten-mile race. Encouraged by her husband and friends, she agreed to and did complete the ten-mile race.

Immediately following that success, the same friends encouraged her to run a "half marathon" race they were running in two months later. Still somewhat unconfident, she verbally committed to running this race. Instantly, Nia regretted committing because she didn't really see the purpose of running nor did she believe she could do it.

Being a lady of her word, however, she attempted to sign up at the last possible moment only to find out that the half marathon was sold out. To keep her commitment to her friends, she signed up for the full marathon (26.2 miles) figuring she can just quit halfway.

Somewhere in her heart, a still small voice constantly urged her to train with confidence. Nia eventually started to feel that she actually may be able to run the full marathon. Her usually supportive husband and friends told her she was crazy. One week before her race, the Chicago marathon had a young thirty-year-old, a trained runner, collapse and die. Family and friends alike made every effort to discourage this young mother of three to NOT run in the marathon. Up to the very moment of the first step of the race, the discouragement continued. Fortunately, Nia's drive would not be hampered.

The day of the race, Nia's husband acquiesced his lack of support and requested to be informed of the location of the finish line. Nia also learned that the course would be shut down in six hours and thirty minutes. There were computers at the starting line to help runners predict their running time based on previous races. Based on her previous race, her predicted finish time would be six hours and forty-seven minutes. Nia was horrified that she would make this tremendous effort to finish and be stopped short of her goal of finishing because the course closed down. Nonetheless, with no more time for fretting, Nia set out for the finish line.

Most races have people who volunteer to be pacers. Pacers wear their predicted finish times in big letters on their backs so neophyte runners can hook up with someone whose running time is compatible with theirs. Right in front of Nia was a lady named Jill whose pace time was five hours. Nia thought she would keep pace with Jill for as long as possible. This would help push her a little in the beginning so that she would finish in the allotted six-and-a-half hours.

Ironically, this was Jill's first marathon too. She was ecstatic to have someone to run with her. She had signed up with a group who was running for a charity, and the officials paced everyone in this group the same. Prior to the start, Jill and Nia were exchanging stories about all the criticisms they had each received about the craziness of this adventure. They had forged an immediate bond sharing positive affirmations and encouragements to help each other.

At the halfway mark, Nia and Jill were only six minutes off of the halfway goal mark of two and a half hours. Here were two strangers who were committed to an accomplishment, both without intense training and support for this goal. They sailed together totally committed to making it to the finish line. By seventeen miles, Nia was in pain. Every step was an effort. Amazingly, Jill picked up a second wind, and it was like Nia became one with Jill and together, these two unprepared, inexperienced women finished the race in five hours and twenty-eight minutes. Jill ran five paces ahead of Nia for the last five miles. At the finish line, Jill slowed down to grab Nia's hand and together arms held high they finished the race.

If you were to ask Jill, she would tell you she could not have finished without Nia because the first half was really hard. How do two women, full of faith, with different motivations for completing a twenty-six-mile race, never done by either before, find each other in a crowd of thousands and do what everyone told them was impossible?

Are You Listening?

Jessica, a junior in high school, was found crying hysterically upon her mother's arrival home from work. Just last week her cell phone was stolen, and now her iPod had been taken while she was taking a math test. Over 200 iPods had been stolen from students at this high school in the last six months. The suspects were the three girls that sat surrounding her desk, but authorities could not see any iPods on the girls, and without search warrants, their purses could not be inspected.

After Jessica had calmed down, she went to a chat room of her high school friends and somebody said that she saw Erica Hoover take the iPod from Jessica's purse. Jessica related this information to her mother at the family dinner table. Erica was a loner, so no one knew where she lived. Just then, Angela, Jessica's twelve-year-old sister mentioned that a boy with the same last name of Hoover had boarded her bus last week.

She knew his name because he was on the wrong bus and the bus driver had asked for his name to make a report. Angela was sitting in the front seat of the bus and overheard it. The bus driver dropped him off at his house before his other stops since it was on the way.

Angela piped in that she remembered where he lived. This amazed the family because, according to her mother, Angela doesn't pay attention to anything going on around her. However, this boy with the same last name as the alleged iPod thief lived on the main street over a gas station. According to Angela, they immediately knew where he lived because there was only one place in town that had living quarters over a garage.

Jessica's father immediately went to the Hoover family apartment and pressed the mother into talking with Erica. Erica ultimately gave up Jessica's iPod she had stolen and a cell phone that had been taken earlier from someone else. Naturally, Jessica was elated. Since her father had seen other stolen iPods at this house, the police were able to get a search warrant. Many cell phones and iPods were recovered thanks to that little detail provided to Angela by God through her sister! Are you listening?

War Miracle

In 1945, Josef Kupfermunz, a prisoner in a Jewish concentration camp, was part of a mass prisoner train transfer by the Nazis. This was an effort to quickly move out the last of the prisoners from Auschwitz before the anticipated arrival of the American Liberation soldiers. There were 300 prisoners on Josef's train. Their destination was the Garmisch Partenkirchen Mountains, where the Nazis plan was to use machine guns to kill the prisoners—who were the last evidence of the Nazi extermination of the Jews.

The Red Cross had provided survival kits to the concentration camps over the years but they were never distributed to the prisoners. Instead they were stockpiled by the Nazis. In an effort to clean out any evidence of Nazi brutality and to show the Nazis had issued the kits, each prisoner was issued a Red Cross package as they boarded the ill-fated passenger trains.

Josef's ten-car train was extremely crowded so Josef hung his Red Cross package on the emergency brake to keep it safe and out of the way. Unbeknownst to him, that hanging Red Cross kit had somehow jammed the brake system of the entire train. The jammed brakes had prevented the train from leaving the station at its scheduled time. One and a half days passed before the cause of the delay was discovered and removed.

It took twenty-four hours for the train to reach the mountains. As the train rolled to a stop, Josef heard the sound of machine gun fire. The machine gun fire was a result of the Nazis lining up all of the passengers from the train ahead of Josef's. The Nazis were shooting them as quickly as possible as the American Liberation soldiers were already in the near small town less than a mile away. Suddenly, the shooting had stopped. The dazed passengers in Josef's train disembarked the train. No Germans with guns were there. The day and a half delay from the Red Cross package Josef had hung on a lever had saved every passenger on that train from deadly extermination in perfect timing.

This story was relayed to me by Josef's grandson Sol as I was sitting next to him on an air flight. Sol had missed the flight before this one. Another delay in the Kupfermunz family so that this parable could be told to the world.

Tough Love

Karen's thirty-five-year-old son has been in the jail system since he was seventeen years old for drug and alcohol abuse which probably explains why her neighbors, Jim and Linda, gravitated to her when their son Jerry entered a drug treatment program at fourteen.

If any of you have had this experience, you know that without "tough love" you most likely would never have made it through this process. In fact, those who have successfully made it through the painful process of admitting their son or daughter is an alcoholic or drug addict learn that the process is just as much about the parents evolving into changed people as it is about their child learning new skills to cope with the reasons why they attached themselves to drugs and alcohol to begin with. It is always easier to get counseling and guidance from someone who has been there. Jim was having a particularly hard time dealing with his son's addiction since, for Jim, the sun rose and set around young Jerry.

Whenever Jim was at his rope's end and ready to give up and acquiesce to Jerry's pleas to be released prematurely from his treatment center, he would call Karen for support. One day Karen decided to verbally chronicle for Jim her son Randy's seventeen-year ordeal with substance abuse. She started from the beginning when Randy was thirteen and finished a fifth of Southern Comfort with two friends in one night. Karen always felt it was just a "stage" Randy was going through to help him cope with his parents' divorce and the death of his sister when he was young. Karen closed the conversation with Jim asking him if that was what he wanted to see for Jerry. Randy's epic story was all Jim needed to hear to keep him on track to remain in his tough love stance. Jim had come to heavily rely on Karen's strength when his own would wane.

One day Jim was preparing to meet his ex-wife (Jerry's mom) Beth in court. Beth was not in agreement with Jerry's treatment and used every resource in her power to fight Jerry's confinement. Beth was a druggie herself. The cost to keep Jerry in treatment was $10,000/month. Jim had borrowed $60,000 to pay for Jerry's treatment, not to mention the $20,000 in legal fees he had spent so far to fight Beth to keep Jerry in treatment. Jim had tried to contact Karen the day before the court hearing regarding this very issue for some words of encouraging strength, but she was out of the country and could not be reached.

Jim wondered if he was doing the right thing fighting Beth any longer. After all, she was Jerry's mother. Was Jim vindictive over the divorce from seven years ago? Could Jerry really be helped, or did the treatment center just want Jim's money? Was Jerry really a drug addict? Jim was beside himself, covered in doubt about the whole situation as he made his way up the courthouse steps. Who does he run into waiting outside the courtroom for his hearing with the judge? Randy, Karen's son.

Randy was in court for his seventh drunk driving charge. Jim could see that Randy was conning everyone, including himself, about his alcohol addiction. Jim confirmed for himself everything Karen had told him about what could happen to his son if his son's substance abuse continued as he listened to Randy's tales of woe when it came to describing the negative details of his life.

Seeing Randy rekindled Jim's fire to continue the battle to do what he intuitively knew was in Jerry's best interest, regardless of the cost or the chaos. He received the best picture of Jerry's future if he didn't see Jerry's treatment through. What were the chances?

Jim was seeking in earnest for answers outside himself when Randy appeared. Soul can and will connect you with answers you need when you are willing to remove yourself (your desires, personal feelings, judgment) from the equation.

Mother's Day

It had been fifteen years since Lynn's only child, a daughter, had died of a drug overdose. Since that time, Lynn had volunteered at her church teaching fifth and sixth graders for ten years until her need to help children was sated.

Attending the Mother's Day service at church was always hard for her. When the request for all mothers to stand for a round of applause was heralded, it brought up annual feelings of loss and inadequacy for Lynn. A feeling of limbo as if to say "I birthed a child, but there is no proof of that now. Am I still a mother?" Lynn had learned that part of the healing process for the loss of a child is leaning "into" those vagaries with the heart of a mother, regardless of the emptiness she still felt, so she stood collectively with other mothers as tears streamed like a raging river down her face.

The annual church Bake Sale, a teen group fundraiser, takes place every Mother's Day. At the close of the service, five teenagers, four of them carrying cakes, climbed the stage steps providing a visual to the congregation of all the goodies awaiting their purchase. Four specific cakes were being auctioned off on stage to spark the bake sale. The student not carrying a cake, Romando, a seventeen-year-old, was asked by the minister how long he had been coming to Sunday school. He replied, "Since I was a baby."

Tears began again for Lynn. This time they were the tears of a prideful mother. Romando had been one of Lynn's favorite and prized students from five years ago. In her class for two years, as fifth and sixth grades were combined, she had grown quite fond of him and him of her. He had always made a point to find her in the fellowship hall for a hug on Sundays after service to report to his favorite teacher his dreams, goals, and current school projects.

The minister asked Romando what he was going to study in college and his answer of bio-chemical engineering opened the hearts and pocketbooks of all who heard his words. That four cake auction raised over $3,000. The minister brought Romando up on the stage to show the results of what a good youth program could provide. For Lynn however, God used the presence of Romando to remind her that although her physical daughter may have left this world, her true mothering energy lives on, not only in Romando but countless other kids she mentored for ten years as Miss Lynn—Sunday school teacher extraordinaire!

Handel's Messiah

Shirley, a Canadian-born artist from a large metropolitan area, attended Handel's Messiah, an oratorio musical, at a local church upon invitation from a local artist group. Due to a snowstorm, she and her husband arrived late, and the church was packed with no seats to be had. The conductor's assistant, an acquaintance of Shirley's, was walking by and noticed her and summoned her to the front row where she and her husband found a seat. Shirley was only several feet away from the violins and the choir. She later stated that "She was so close and well situated that she felt the orchestra and the choir were performing only for her."

At intermission, a violinist sought her out and related to her that at every concert she always picks an audience member's face to focus on as it gives her a connection to the feedback of the listeners. The violinist thanked Shirley profusely as she described Shirley's face so enjoying the music that she felt like she was playing just for Shirley and that pleased her.

The conductor's assistant overheard this conversation and invited Shirley and her husband to an afterglow party for the orchestra. At the party, Shirley was introduced to the conductor, who in conversation, asked Shirley what she did, and Shirley informed him she was an artist.

The conductor told her they had been searching for two years for a local artist to do a painting for the symphony orchestra's program. She invited them to her studio the following Sunday where the entire committee showed up. They loved her work and showed great excitement in finding her, so they struck a deal for her to design a painting that they could produce for the front of next year's program.

Part of the plan was to hold a special concert just for the unveiling of her painting. Additionally, they had visions of issuing limited edition prints of the painting as a way of melding the art world with the music world.

Shirley added to the story that one month before this happened, her favorite radio station that she always has on when she paints converted from easy listening to classical music. During that month they featured Handel's Messiah with its rich history and the story behind the music. Throughout that month they played many different renditions of it. Because of that, she was able to talk to the conductor and musicians very intelligently and passionately about the music at their meeting. God detail?

The symphony orchestra painting launched Shirley's career to a place beyond her wildest dreams.

It's even hard for this writer to believe that a snowstorm was divinely produced merely to delay Shirley's concert entrance so she could get a front seat, meet the violinist, and ultimately be hired to create a painting that raised $8,000 in a charity auction that took Shirley's career to new heights. I guess the real question is, why not?

Chance Meeting

It took my husband and me several years into our marriage to find a Sunday place of worship we could both agree on. Eventually, we enthusiastically agreed on a little intimate church right in our town, notwithstanding many silent struggles between us over this subject.

One Sunday, about three months into our new church "commitment," Howard was sick. Now, I love our new place of worship, but I still missed the soulful gospel music from where I used to worship. I announced to Howard that since he was ill, I would meander over to my old church and see some friends. I noticed, however, there was a gnawing in my gut. It forced me to ask myself, "What kind of a commitment did you really make?" and "If you are speaking the truth when you tell others how much you like the new church, why aren't you going there?" Consequently, I informed my husband that I was going to "our" church without him after all.

Later in the afternoon, with Howard still convalescing, I trekked over to the local park for a four-mile walk. It was a beautiful fall afternoon. About a half mile into the walk, I spotted a woman walking toward me who appeared to be dancing in a rhythmic step. At first, I suspected she must be listening to an iPod. Her arms were swaying. Her feet seemed to be dancing, and her lips were moving. When I detected no headphones, my anthropological curiosity urged me to engage her in conversation, so I asked, "Are you singing?" She replied, "Yes . . . Amazing Grace."

Amazing Grace is my all-time favorite gospel tune. I asked her if she would sing it for me. After all, if you never ask, how can you receive? She agreed, hesitantly. People were passing by, and she wanted to wait until we were alone. So, while waiting, I struck up a conversation with the famous original question, "Come here often?" She replied that she was trying to "fill herself with affirmations of healing." I asked her if she was physically or emotionally sick and her telling reply was, "I'm trying to figure that out."

All of my training tells me that physical sickness is often a defense against some truth we are emotionally unable or unwilling to accept. So I said, "How about if I trade you what I know about the subject of sickness and how we can heal ourselves for your rendition of Amazing Grace?" She lit up with a resounding, "Yes!"

For thirty minutes, I spoke with her of release and love, polarity and truth. She got it. Whatever I said was exactly what she needed to hear. Her soul-filled rendition of Amazing Grace brought tears to my eyes. It was what I needed to hear as well to be reminded that if you stay faithful to your commitments, your needs and desires—in this case, mine was to hear some soul-filled gospel music—the need will be attended to in ways we cannot even surmise.

We left each other after noting our first names were the same, with a long, healing hug between strangers.

Now that was church!

A Matter of Respect

Janet, president of a twenty-employee company, had noticed that the primary source of the company's cash flow had come to a screeching halt. At the same time, she saw that everyone at the office had become needy and inconsiderate towards each other. Janet decided that as president she had to give one of those "get it together" speeches or else closing the company was inevitable. Knowing what she wanted to say and how she needed to say it to be effective were two separate things. She had waited six days after an altercation that took place (that was the final indicator of the fracture in the teamwork) to schedule a company-wide meeting.

Two hours before the big meeting, Janet still could not put her finger on a clear description of what was lacking in the office to cause such a huge shift in her employees, and consequently the company's profitability. As usual for her, she was waiting for a sign or the right words (God details) to clearly express the message she knew was necessary for her employees to hear. One hour before the scheduled company meeting, she had her usual manicure appointment scheduled with Colleen.

During the manicure, Colleen mentioned that she had just hired a professional dog obedience trainer for her one-year-old Doberman, Jack. Colleen proceeded to tell Janet that the first thing the trainer told Colleen to do was to put a stop to the dog sleeping in her bed. The trainer further explained that a lot of things had to change about her relationship with Jack. The trainer related to Colleen that Jack was out of control because he thought he was Colleen's equal. Sleeping in her bed, running ahead of her all the time, whining for a biscuit when he wanted it instead of when it was good for his owner were all signs of disrespect. The trainer made it clear that if Colleen wanted Jack to be a well-mannered pet, he needed to learn and exhibit respect for his owner.

Janet, just one hour before her company-wide talk, now knew what her employees lacked—respect for themselves, respect for each other, and respect for the company. Janet, enlightened as to what her problem was in a meeting of fewer than five minutes, was able to convey the perfect message to her employees from a position of wisdom rather than that of the anger that had fueled the need for the meeting to begin with.

Yes, God even uses dogs and manicurists in providing messages that complete the details we need or ask for.

Chapter 4

Complicated Details

EVENTS AND EXPERIENCES HAPPEN TO US DAILY. UNLESS THEY BRING pleasure or happiness, we usually are complaining about the pain and suffering they cause. Somewhere, somehow it seems that all circumstances in our lives whether simple or complicated, play roles in the foundation of our future experiences. In fact, after this experience, I hope I never question why things happen the way they do. I will try to always be grateful that there is a power greater than myself controlling my life.

It's December 17 and I am sitting in a courtroom waiting for Mark, my nineteen-year-old son, to come out from behind closed doors. This is a sentencing hearing where he's been told by his attorney that he should just get "time served" and be home for Christmas. I hadn't seen Mark in two years. He had been in jail for ninety-six days on an auto theft charge as he was with a convicted felon who needed a car and decided to steal one. Mark was along for the ride and ended up getting caught. I could have bailed him out at any time, but felt jail might just be the medicine he needed.

Being locked up is a terrifying experience. You don't know how good freedom is until it is taken away from you. Incarceration means you are *always* at the mercy of someone else. Originally in medium security, Mark was found with a "smuggled in" cigarette in his cell and was sent to the "hole" for forty-eight hours as punishment. He was then moved to maximum security with prisoners who were in for violent crimes. The inmate in the cell next to Mark was accused of kidnapping and brutally murdering a twelve-year-old child. Mark's collect calls to me clearly indicated he was at his wit's end and scared to death!

Usually, they conduct sentencing hearings involving prisoners first thing on the docket so they can take the prisoner back to jail and not waste so many man hours of the sheriff's department guarding the prisoners. Two hours later the hearings are not involving the incarcerated anymore, and Mark still hasn't been sentenced, when I overhear someone telling the Judge that Mr. Robinette, Mark's attorney, is still one hour away from getting to the courtroom. The judge is asked if she will wait for his attorney to sentence Mark. Without a thought, she adjourns Mark's hearing for thirty days—meaning thirty more days in jail.

My heart is wrenched. I can only wonder what Mark must be feeling when the bailiff goes back to the holding cell to tell him. I was planning on seeing him for Christmas; maybe try to start our relationship all over again. My conscience haunted me until I finally went two days later to bail him out. I cried while I waited for him to be released and hugged him in an unreturned hug when we met. I hadn't touched him in two years. He was a man now; he had just experienced the ultimate toughness—surviving jail. It was strange having him back in the house after kicking him out two years ago for being so out of control. My husband and I had previously agreed that he could not move back into our home, as we did not wish to deal with the disruptions he had created in our lives. I could not put him back out on the streets where he was living. He would surely not find his way having to cope with being a homeless person. He had burned his bridges with everyone else over the last two years. However, my husband relented, and I brought him home.

At first, Mark was a bit rough and crude. A gnat had higher self-esteem than he did. He didn't have two nickels to rub together, and here he was dependent on a woman whom he has been estranged from for the last two years—his mom! Luckily a friend of mine, after hearing his story, offered him a job because as he put it, "Everyone deserves a second chance." I noticed Mark's stubbornness was ebbing and he was genuinely trying to make an effort to rejoin the world of the free.

As if like some kind of omen, at church services on Christmas Eve, a woman bearing a striking resemblance to Mark's judge sat right next to him during the service. We hoped it was a positive sign. It couldn't possibly be the judge; the world is small but not that small.

The morning of Mark's sentencing hearing thirty days later proved to be a miracle. His attorney, Mr. Robinette, explained to us that typically when a nineteen-year-old is involved in a crime such as his, the prosecutor's office offers to put the defendant into a probationary type program. Basically, if the defendant keeps his nose clean for twenty-four months, the charges are dropped. However one of the conditions of this program is that the defendant has no "priors." Several weeks before the car theft incident, Mark got into a fight with the driver of another car and broke out his car window. This misdemeanor qualified as a "prior." Robinette further explained to us in the hallway that due to this misdemeanor, the program was absolutely out of the question. Mark did not qualify. He was explaining further that Mark's best shot at avoiding any future jail time would be to plead guilty to a five-year felony and in turn, the prosecutor's office would request that the judge accept "time served" as final retribution. Most likely, however, there would still be more jail time.

Just at that moment, the prosecutor handling this case walked by. Robinette pulled him off to the side and explained the situation regarding the program for nineteen-year-olds and the fact that Mark should plead guilty. I began to tell the prosecutor that I did not feel justice would be served any better by sending Mark back to jail, and I felt that his recent time spent there had made an impact on him in a positive direction. I explained that Mark had been living on the street for two years. Robinette told him that in all his years he had never really seen a parent leave their kid in jail who said they would like I did. I told him further that Mark had signed up to go back to school, has a job, and it seems that he really wants to turn his life around. The prosecutor said that there wasn't much he could do because of the "prior" and that this particular judge was adamant about the "no priors" rule. Waiting our turn in the courtroom, Mark and I hoped for the best. Mark commented when the Judge came out that he was sure it was the woman who sat next to him in church on Christmas Eve. Did God give us a sign?

The prosecuting attorney came up to me and asked if I was the same person who testified in the Fred Luna murder trial some years back. Replying yes, he reminded me that he was the prosecutor in that case. Fred Luna was my immediate neighbor who had axed his wife to death. Luna's defense was that his wife was dating another man and he went crazy when he found out. The prosecutor saw it differently, and we met for lunch before the trial to crystalize my testimony. I'm sure he remembered how hard that trial was for me. All the memories it brought back! All of a sudden, the prosecuting attorney had taken a whole new interest in Mark. I saw him and Robinette reviewing a book that tells what sentences go with what crimes. They were earnestly trying to find a different solution to Mark's problem. Robinette had come to sit by us as we awaited our turn. He indicated further that although they tried there was still nothing they could do to change the five-year felony plea.

He asked me in front of Mark what happened to him, for it seemed that he was a nice boy with a loving mom. With tears in my eyes, I stated that fourteen years ago to the day, my daughter had been hit by a car and died and that Mark was a witness to it. Ever since that event, Mark became hardened and stubborn. I suggested it was a wall he had erected to cover the pain of such a substantial loss in his life. Mark had tears in his eyes when I hugged him and told him that maybe it is time to let it go and move on. I suggested that his life doesn't need to be so empty any longer; that he is loved. Then Robinette asked me about the Luna murder. I told him that this event might very well have been even more detrimental to my son than his sister's death. I had to identify the body, and the police never told me she had been killed with an ax. It was a grueling, horrible thing to see. A sight I shall never forget. I was emotionally comatose for a good many months during which time Mark's father made a fervent pitch for custody of Mark. Unable to cope with anything, I let Mark move in with his dad without much of a fight, which I'm sure it indicated to Mark that I didn't care about him— furthering his emotional loss. Robinette, with tears in his eyes, admitted that Mark has been through some tough times. It seemed Robinette's spirit had been touched.

Just before we were called, a prisoner in jail blues was before the judge. He was accused of armed robbery and had already served seven months in jail before this sentencing. His "weapon" consisted of his hand wrapped up in a towel to look like a gun. The judge gave him a two-year sentence for stealing seventy-two dollars which had been returned to the victim. Mark had stolen a vehicle worth many thousands. Was he to expect the same treatment? The anxiety was intense. We then heard "People vs. Mark," my pulse quickened, and I wished Mark good luck. After that, a peacefulness came over me. The judge noticed in the file that Mark was nineteen and he had a prior and asked Robinette what he might have to say. Robinette jokingly said to the judge, "With a prior will it do any good to even ask?" The judge laughed back and said, "No!" Then, as if moved by spirit, Robinette said, "Seriously your honor, this boy has had a unique, rough life." He went on to reiterate the sister's death, the next door neighbor's murder and Mark living on the streets for the last two years. He also added that Mark is going back to school and has a job.

He then turned around and pointed to me. He told the judge that I had left him in jail for ninety-eight days, even though I had the money to spring him. He said that he had never defended a kid whose parents actually left their kid in jail when they said they would. He mentioned that I was a caring mom and wanted Mark to learn what the results of a life of crime would be. He also stated that he believed Mark was showing a change in his life, and maybe he needed one more chance! The prosecutor agreed that this was a unique case and that some leniency might be in order. Then, as if by some miracle, the judge, after asking Mark several rote questions, stated that she was going to put him on the probation program we had so hoped for. But she also was stern enough to tell him that if he violates any of the rules, she will sentence him for his crime. Robinette and Mark were elated. Robinette said that he could not believe that this has happened. He pointed out that it was a good thing he was late for court back in December because it would not have worked out this way. He would not have had the chance to talk to me and learn the things about Mark that he discovered today, and that the same prosecuting attorney would not have been available to us at that time.

I agreed with Robinette regarding the Divine timing of the December event. I stated that his lateness gave me an opportunity to show Mark that I really loved and cared about him to have pulled him out of jail in time for Christmas. Something I think he needed to be shown. Robinette, still feeling the spirit, turned to Mark and told him that he had not taken on any court-appointed cases (which Mark's was) in years. It was only by accident that he answered the phone in his office when the court called and asked for one of the other attorneys in his office to represent Mark. He further stated that his standard fee for this type of representation would run between $5,000 and $7,500. He scratched his head and said this whole thing had been a miracle. He lovingly told Mark how he must change his life because these "SECOND CHANCE MIRACLES JUST DON'T HAPPEN." Oh, this wasn't the end.

When I went to the judge's clerk to retrieve the bond money, I asked the clerk after naming my church if the Judge also went there. She stated yes. I then described the man that was with the woman who sat next to Mark on Christmas Eve. Sure enough, it was the judge! I praise God for this truly magnificent example of Divine timing and miracles.

Complicated details are easy for God. Following are other complicated details to prove it.

HRC

Carol, a real estate broker, was raised in a Bible-based church. As a result, she made it a personal mission to bring the messages of the Bible to others. In fact, Carol gave me my first Bible. She became the "go to" person for her sphere of influence when someone wanted more information about the Bible.

In May of 1985, three of us got together at Carol's house on a Thursday morning and committed to meeting every Thursday morning forevermore to study the Bible. And so it was. It became known as the "Holy Roller Club" (HRC).

The HRC quickly grew to eleven ladies with very diverse backgrounds in both religion and career. This, of course, led to various conversations and spirit-stimulated ideas—which was the true purpose of our class.

Beverly, a massage therapist who began her practice making house calls, had just opened her own health spa right around the corner from our weekly class. One of our group, Liz, brought Beverly to our class for the first time, which brought our group to twelve. Twelve is a very complete, spiritual number.

It didn't take long for all of us to fall in love with Beverly. Her spirit was so loving and gentle. She always had a kind word for everyone. Her smile was constant and sent shards of light to all of us. She put her whole heart into sharing with our class her experiences and ideas. This whole-heartedness was also how she did her massages.

Not long after she joined us, Beverly revealed that she had lost a twelve-year-old son who had drowned fifteen years ago. Her pain was still evident when she told his story. It was then that I felt immediately kindred to her, for I too shared the experience of the loss of a child.

Beverly was only with us for four months when she shared with us that doctors just discovered she had pancreatic cancer. Apparently, her type of pancreatic cancer was rapid-moving, so her doctors immediately prescribed an infusion pump which injected chemotherapy directly into her pancreas 24/7. Unfortunately, her health insurance did not cover this type of treatment. The situation put undue stress on Beverly and her family.

Somebody in our Bible study class came up with the idea to put on a fundraiser to help pay the thousands of dollars that insurance did not pay for Beverly's treatment. What happened next was nothing short of a miracle!

Within forty-five days, twelve ladies with absolutely no fundraising experience raised over $10,600 by hosting a benefit at a local park complete with kid games and prizes, face painting, hot air balloon rides, food, and beverages. Everything was donated. The HRC prayed every Thursday for those six weeks between the idea and event culmination.

Beverly passed about sixty days after the fundraiser. However, I'll never forget her speech in a weakened condition at the event. She expressed that she had never felt such love as she did from the eleven women who were, up to six months ago, complete strangers. She was happy that her husband would have some of the financial burden lifted from him from her medical expenses. She mentioned how amazing God is to use cancer to bring so many people together for one cause.

I was the person who received the idea. At every turn, everything was provided. The "worker bees" were provided. T-shirts by a local auto dealership were donated, and a local restaurant catered the food. The hot-air balloon, our biggest and most visible attraction that brought people in, was also donated. Signs, paper products, everything. Complicated details? Maybe. Being in the experience of God providing answers to every need is a most exhilarating experience.

Finally Put Together

My husband, for a holiday gift one year, bought me some stones (crystals) along with a primer book on crystals. I immediately became a fan of crystals and their energy and began studying everything I could get my hands on about crystals. I was mostly interested in how stones/crystals are formed, where they come from, the difference between agates, quartz, chert, etc. I searched the web, looking to get the data I wanted.

Six months after the gift, I was reorganizing my resource books and lo and behold, I found a book titled *The Ultimate Stone Healer's Guide*. It was one of many resource books I had owned for years. When I read that book long ago, I had highlighted it in many places. The highlights from then provided amazing insight into the crystals. From that, I started writing a manual about stones . . . all from receiving four simple crystals as a gift. In further reorganizing, I discovered I had seven other books that were related to crystals, how they are formed, how they heal, etc. Some of these books I had read over twenty-five years ago. Most provided exact pieces of information I was looking for to further my research. Simple, yet complicated details over a great span of time collecting until the time was right for me to "sew" them into a comprehensive crystal guide.

How does that happen? Take some time to recognize a "God" detail similar to this in your life. That is, what have you learned or been prepared to do or accomplish in the past that you can take to the next level that is staring you in the face now? Nothing we do or learn is by chance. God delivers details that linger in our lives until the big picture is finally puzzled together. A person you meet, a class you took, the neighborhood you live in, etc. Are you paying attention to where you are being led?

Soul Contract

One can never be sure about the contract our Soul makes before we incarnate into human form. This subject would take another book. However, you can be sure that without question, the contract your Soul makes on your behalf is always about smoothing your edges, bringing light (healing energy) to someone, or aiding in planetary evolution. Here's how Heidi's Soul must have agreed to make a difference with God in every detail.

In October of 2006, Heidi was diagnosed with B-Cell Lymphoma. She had the majority of her small bowel removed followed by extensive chemotherapy. She was amazingly cheerful and upbeat as she lost all of her hair, could not clean her house (for her, a passion), or work because of the lethargy the chemo treatments triggered. In September of 2007, Heidi's father, Jack, himself taking chemotherapy for a different type of cancer, died suddenly from an automobile accident on his way to the doctor.

Jack had a brother named Joe. Joe's wife, Irene, and Heidi's mother, Doreen, had not spoken to each other in at least twenty years. Doreen never did understand why her husband's brother's wife never liked her. Although Irene did not come to her brother-in-law Jack's funeral, her three children did. Heidi and her three cousins joyfully reunited. They promised to keep her in their prayers and hold positive thoughts about her successful cancer recovery. Less than a week later, Heidi received a package from her Aunt Irene, whom she too had been estranged from for twenty years. In the package was a medallion called the Miraculous Medal, which Aunt Irene had had blessed by Pope John XXIII many years before, along with a prayer card explaining the Miraculous Medal. Did I mention Heidi was exceptionally religious? (This, by the way, is not necessary for God to appear in the details of your life). Heidi immediately attached a chain to the precious metal, so lovingly sent, and wore it around her neck. It brought her more profound faith and comfort in dealing with her cancer.

Heidi sent a thank you note to Irene for sending her the medal. About this time, Heidi's mother, Doreen found a journal from 1953 where she had written, "I really like Irene. I wish she lived closer so I could visit her every day." After reading that journal, she decided to write to her sister-in-law expressing the love she had felt for Irene all those years ago. This gesture opened up new pathways and opportunities, which they took, and reunited their loving relationship.

A family reunited by the path cancer took them on. The details all handled by God.

Death Details

Ten years ago, after much pleading, my husband Bill finally convinced me to go on a cruise. We traveled on the MS Westerdam— a beautiful ship. Little did I know that some years into the future, on a newer ship with the exact name, I would finally bid my Billy good-bye.

We were in Jamaica the day before he passed where we had climbed the beautiful ten-story Dunn's River Falls. At first, I thought if I had only seen the picture someone took of us after the climb, I would have known he was going to die. His face was all bloated, the first sign that some of his organs were shutting down. As a matter of fact, there were a lot of other signs that his death was imminent; I just wasn't paying attention.

If you don't believe that animals carry messages skip these next few paragraphs. Several days before our cruise I flew down to Florida to be with some friends who had been married for less than thirty days. I didn't know our friend's new wife Linda very well, so she and I spent a lot of time walking and talking in my three-day solo visit. During our outings, we experienced two animal incidents which were clear indicators of a significant change to come.

First, was the turkey vulture (often called buzzards). Everywhere we walked, and we put in a good twenty-five miles, turkey vultures flew over our heads. Even on one of the houses across the street from their home, a turkey vulture was sunning himself every time we walked by. We stood in awe of his magnificence with his wings wide open as if to say come into my arms—I will comfort you. Linda and I both knew the vultures were a sign of something; they were everywhere we went.

In the same three day period, we had the most breathtaking visit from a mother raccoon and her four baby raccoons. According to Indian folklore, the raccoon, because of its mask (disguise), suggests transformation is on the way. This mother pranced her beautiful family right through the backyard, circling two trees right outside the large window where we just happened to be sitting.

I remember Linda attending our bon voyage and whispering in my ear, "Be sure to let me know what you think the vultures and raccoons were telling you." It would be four days later, and the whole world would know. My Billy had a heart attack in our stateroom, while I was getting a massage.

When I tell people "My husband died while we were on a cruise" their first response is always, "How awful!" However, if you could pick your time to die and you were in the middle of the Caribbean in your bathing suit, wouldn't you choose that? I know it would have been my Billy's first choice. No fuss, no muss.

I had suspected there was some physical degeneration going on as Bill was losing things, missing our exit on the expressway, and forgetting the simplest of details. He was also becoming exceptionally mean and crabby. He knew he had diabetes but would not treat it. In fact, Bill hadn't been to a doctor for fifteen years. A doctor himself, he tried to holistically treat a disease that eventually has its way with you.

The second night of our final cruise we had a very stupid altercation. By then he had probably been to the dining room dessert table five times since we embarked. He became very mean and insulting (most unlike the kind man I married), so I opted not to join him for dinner that night. He refused to apologize to me for his unkind remarks, and I did not want to be in his space.

About forty-five minutes after he left for dinner, an amazing thing happened. The room steward came into our room to turn down the bed. His sweetness filled the room! He politely asked why I wasn't at dinner, and I told him my husband had hurt my feelings. Without missing a beat, he said, "I'm sorry Mum." Immediately some voice in my head said: "Alright, you got your apology, now forgive and move on." When Bill returned from dinner and came to bed I hugged him and fell asleep. The remaining two days with my husband before he died were filled with the sweetness of my Billy from years past. How different those two days would have been without the urge to forgive— provided to me by the kindness of the room steward who offered the apology I wanted.

God's perfect detailing of my husband's passing continued. On Thursday morning after some sweet, intimate moments we decided to "dress" for breakfast and go to the dining room rather than the usual breakfast buffet. We had only done that one other time during our seven other cruises together. While dressing, I remember looking at the phone and seeing a little red button with 911 on it. I even had a thought about how stupid that was. Can't people just dial 9-1-1? Little did I know God was providing a detail that I was subconsciously storing for use less than twelve hours later.

After breakfast, we donned our bathing suits and off to the sundeck we went. I knew something wasn't right when Bill said he didn't want lunch because breakfast had him not feeling well. I teased him a little, kissed him goodbye, and then I went to lunch and for a massage. That was the last time I saw my Billy alive.

He died three hours before I found him laying on the bed right next to the phone that had the handy little 911 button. Thank God! I was so distraught to see him lifeless, and it was all I could do to press that little red button in the dark room. I had not turned the lights on because I thought he was napping. It was time to get ready to go to dinner, and when I gently pushed his chest to awaken him, I instantly knew he was gone. The only thing I saw in my mind's eye was the location of that silly little red 911 button.

In the ship's infirmary, one of its officers told me that according to maritime law, the legal officials of the next port-of-call has authority over any "events" such as death, that occur on a ship between ports. Our next port was Mexico. The officer told me that quite possibly they would remove my husband and myself for investigative purposes because they can. The officer indicated that he was already e-mailing back and forth to advise the officials at the Mexican port that there was no cause for their investigation as their doctor reported that Bill died of natural causes. I was in too much shock to be concerned at the time, but weeks later I was told of a woman whose husband died of natural causes while on vacation in Mexico. It cost her ten days and $24,000 to get her and her deceased husband's body out of Mexico and back home.

Imagine my surprise the next day when I heard the Captain over the loudspeaker regretfully inform the passengers that we would not be stopping in the Mexican port due to high winds making it impossible to bring the ship into port. I remember looking down over the balcony thinking, "That's odd! We're on a brand new giant ship; I don't even see white caps in the water." The Captain's announcement was another of God's most wonderful details in action. We avoided any problems that might have occurred if we stopped in Mexico with Bill's body.

The cruise line was marvelous. The staff moved me into a suite. The steward who took me to my new room commented on how they never have a vacancy of these rooms but was glad they were able to provide me with one now. They also comped me on any phone calls I needed to make. At fifteen dollars per minute, that was most generous of them. I called several people and left my number. Amazingly not one person who tried calling me back was able to get through. God's attention to this detail was most important because at least fifteen people told me they attempted to call but could never get a connection. And may I say "Thank God!" Those three days of solitude were a definite blessing to me. I didn't have to describe what happened to anyone. Every four hours or so I would go to the internet on my terms and respond to the fifteen to twenty emails I received. I cried and cried and cried, but I had a chance to feel my loss in total peace and quiet with schools of dolphins (a rare sighting I've since learned) frequently appearing to me in the middle of the ocean bringing me, yet again, another animal message: breathe. Due to the physical shock I was experiencing, I had to force myself to breathe. Dolphins transcend the upper (air) and lower (water) worlds with their ability to survive in both. It was a gentle kind of reminder to me of what my husband must have been going through as well—transcending both worlds.

Even writing this now, months after his passing, I am still in awe over how every detail of this experience was divinely guided. Our next port of call was Key West, the good ole US of A. We left from Fort Lauderdale so we would be disembarking from there as well. As I saw it, I only had to deal with two practical issues. The first, what to do with my husband's body. The second, what to do with his car since he drove in from Michigan and I had flown.

When I decided to make some inquiring phone calls, I took my phone and Billy's phone to get the numbers I needed. I noticed two voice messages remained on my phone that I received but never responded to while on land four days before we left. One was from Patricia, a client of mine who owns a funeral home that I had for sale. The other was from Bob, a boating captain who was a longtime friend. At the time I received Bob's call, I thought it exceptionally strange. Bob's message was, "Hi! Brought a boat to Fort Lauderdale, and if you're in the area call me." His phone number followed. I never called him back. I have no idea why I saved these two voice messages (I probably received twenty while I was in Florida those four days). I immediately called Pat from the funeral home. She remarkably handled every single detail regarding Bill's body. My husband's ashes arrived home about five days after I did.

What I didn't understand when I first received Bob's text message was that he physically brought a boat down from Michigan to Florida, through the waterways. He clarified that later when I called him from the ship. I learned he was without wheels to get back to Michigan, and in an instant, my only two problems were handled. I'm still in amazement at how the resolution to those problems had been put into place before I knew I was even going to need them. God's details continued.

I asked Jan, our friend, to round up our gang to come to our house on Sunday night which was the day of my return flight. I thought it best for everyone to hear about Bill's passing at one time. My flight was two hours late, and I had this horrible vision of my friends sitting in the driveway for two hours in the freezing December weather because Bill, due to his trust issues, would never leave a spare key with anyone. Little did I know that he placed a key in the neighbor's mailbox before he left with a sticky note that said: "Just in case." Jan just assumed that our neighbors would have a key and retrieved it from them.

When I came home, it was to beautiful music, lit candles, and a stunning food display. But more importantly, our loving friends were all there to hear the details of our loss all at one time. It was nice to share our grief together. It was at this gathering that my neighbor

George told us of a drive Bill had over the past three months to seal, caulk, paint, repair, and finish up all of the projects that he had wanted to get to for the last three years. As I recall, he did seem to complain a lot about all the work he was doing around the house. I remember commenting to him as he was putting on six coats of paint on our newly finished fireplace. I said, "Stop and relax. You can finish when we come back from the cruise." Procrastination was the norm for Bill, but not this time. And so it was that our house was left in perfect order for me. Another detail attended to.

My husband's only vestige of independence was his checkbook. Only his name was on it. I never knew where he kept it and just saw it on Sundays when he would write out his tithe to the church. When I walked into our home office the night I flew home, it was the only thing that I found on his desk, and the very last check in the book was signed.

That night George also told me that Bill cleaned the attic out while I was out of town, three weeks before our cruise. My husband, the perennial pack rat, had managed to cram so much stuff in the attic that it was stuffed from top to bottom, side to side and front to back with everything under the sun. I assumed George meant that Bill had just created a pathway through the junk—his usual method of cleaning things out. I went up to the attic two weeks after he passed and was brought to my knees in tears. I always joked about how I would haunt him if he ever left me with that horrible attic to clean out. The "cleaned out" attic contained the following items: two pieces of luggage, four coolers, and five plastic storage boxes. That's it.

Bill and I taught Sunday school at our church. He was in the three-year-old room for close to seven years. A perfect spot for him as he never had children of his own. Some of those three-year-olds loved Bill so much that they would not leave his room when they turned four until he would sit with them for several Sundays in their new classroom. Quite a testament to who he really was, I might add. One little girl was almost five before she would leave. She and her mother attended his funeral service. During the ceremony, mom and daughter took the podium and told the following story:

"As you may or may not be aware, I have been going through a very nasty divorce for over a year. One of the only stabilities in my daughter's life was Mr. Bill. She finally was willing to leave his room in September because at five-years-old, she started Kindergarten, and I convinced her she needed to move on to kindergarten at church too. Because of the divorce, my daughter had not slept entirely through the night in a year, but instead, she would wake up screaming from bad dreams. That all changed over a week ago.

"She told me that she had a dream of schools of dolphins surrounding her. My daughter's exact words were: 'Mr. Bill came to me swimming with the dolphins. He hugged me and told me everything was good. Only think of these dolphins when you are sad, and you will be happy again.' It has been nine days since Mr. Bill came to my daughter in her dream and my daughter has fully slept through the night since."

God's hand continued in every imaginable detail. Due to the timing of his death, December 1, I was able to grieve along with the planet at a time where things hibernate and are physically preparing for the rebirth that is awaiting us all in the spring. As it was, as if to attend to the final details of Billy's passing, that spring, our regular nesting swans (another animal message indicating new power is on the way) produced seven (the number of God) cygnets for my personal enjoyment that aided in my grief recovery.

Three weeks before we went on the cruise, I purchased a guided journaling book as a gift for a longtime friend I was meeting for lunch one Sunday who was moving to Utah. I forgot to bring it to our farewell luncheon and left it in the cupboard of my Sunday School Class. I just "happened" to find it two weeks after Billy passed and brought it home. It was when I opened it shortly thereafter, that I received the idea to write *Sacred Grief.* The rest is history.

Every detail needed for our lives is already planned out. What we do with those details is another matter. The more we recognize them and give thanks for them, the more we will receive them. Life is so much easier and calmer when we can fully comprehend that God's hand is in every detail.

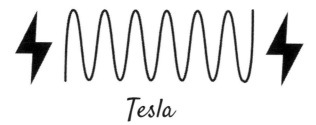

Tesla

Nikola Tesla was born in 1856 in Serbia. Although his name is fittingly known for representing a high-end electric car, few people realize his importance in taking Thomas Edison's invention of direct current electricity (DC) to the next level with his invention of alternate current (AC) electricity, without which appliance motors and even cell phones and computers would be unable to perform.

Edison's DC electricity was not able to "safely" travel any distance and therefore could not be trusted. The details of Tesla's invention of AC electricity are an amazing example of how God supplied every detail to Tesla from birth on so that he was prepared to evolve Edison's original invention.

Tesla's mother was a famous inventor of weaving machines. His father was a priest of the Serbian Orthodox church. Exceptionally bright at a young age, his father had grand plans for him to join the priesthood. Because of this plan, Tesla's father required his son to read and memorize long passages of religious text in preparation for his future. In Serbia, at that time in history, the choice of careers for young men was either military service or the priesthood.

At seventeen Nikola contracted cholera, an often fatal bacterial disease of the small intestine. His immune system was most likely compromised by the depression that set in when his father forbade him to go to the electrical engineering college he had prepared so hard to attend in lieu of the seminary. Recognizing Nikola was dying, his father agreed to send him to technical school if he recovered, which he did almost instantly. That was 1873. Edison made the first demonstration of his incandescent light bulb in December 1879.

In 1884, when Tesla was twenty-eight, he went to New York. Soon thereafter, Tesla noticed a spectacular sunset that recalled in his mind one of those long, religious passages his father forced him to memorize. Somehow, a combination of the passage and the sun setting formulated in his mind a schematic concept of the circular power of energy. He immediately took a stick and drew this concept in the dirt, which eventually evolved into his AC invention in 1888. When Tesla presented his AC theory to Edison, Edison promptly rejected Tesla's theory causing Tesla to ultimately hook up with a man named Westinghouse, and the rest is history.

Could this invention have had happened if he hadn't been forced to memorize these religious passages? If he didn't have "inventor DNA" passed down from his mother? If he hadn't contracted cholera, an extremely rare and often fatal bacterial disease of the small intestine, he would have been forced to attend seminary. Instead, God sent cholera to Nikola to change his father's heart.

Tesla was an inventor and futurist but indeed not a businessman. Having been a gambler and prone to depression, he died penniless. However, his Soul carried the mission to see to the invention of alternate current electricity through a fantastic series of complicated God details.

God sees to the evolution of our planet. God uses all of us, our birth, our culture, our career choices, etc., to execute the details of the evolution. Most of us are unwilling to listen and follow the decisions laid out for us. Aren't we glad Tesla did?

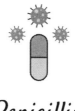

Penicillin

Throughout history, infections have been the real culprit of death in war battles, far outpacing death caused by actual battle injuries. The discovery of penicillin changed all that, but not without many people, global connections, and God details.

In 1928, after having returned from vacation, a Londoner named Alexander Fleming noticed a green mold called Penicillium notatum contaminated and or killed off some of the bacteria he was growing in petri dishes in his lab. A further microscopic study by Fleming showed that the mold was also preventing the growth of the staphylococci bacteria, a bacteria responsible for severe infection and often death.

More research ensued, and Dr. Fleming concluded that something in that green mold was antagonistic to the growth of bacteria. Fleming lacked the resources needed to heighten his investigation further. However, he did write an article that subsequently was published in the British Journal of Environmental Pathology. In the fourteen years between Dr. Fleming's "accidental" discovery and its civilian use, a myriad of God's details took place to ensure that this new miracle drug, a turning point in medical history, went to market.

Dr. Howard Florey, a professor of pathology at Oxford University, just "happened" upon the article Dr. Fleming wrote when rifling through his piles of old, unread journals. As a result, and with resources and staff at his disposal, Dr. Florey eventually produced a series of mold cultures confirming Fleming's discovery, but was faced with the issue of producing the mold on a scale large enough that could be helpful to many, rather than a few. It took 2,000 liters of mold culture to obtain enough penicillin to treat just one case of sepsis successfully.

In 1941, just before the United States entered World War II, Florey's team went to Illinois to work with scientists in an attempt to mass produce this new wonder drug.

While Florey and his team were still in Illinois, a lab assistant, Mary Hunt, brought in a melon covered in a pretty, "golden" mold. This species of fungus, Penicillium chrysogenum, turned out to yield 200 times that of its relative and even more when altered with X-ray, filtration, and other enhancement modalities.

From an accidental (or was it?) discovery, a casual flipping-through of dated medical journals by a well-endowed laboratory, and a transatlantic connection with a moldy, golden orbed melon came the development of an antibiotic that transcended any previously known cures for a most debilitating bacteria. God Detail? I should say so!

Author Guidance

During the writing process of *Sacred Grief* one Friday morning while still in bed, I received the idea to add a section called "Male Grief." So as any good author would do, I got up, pen and paper in hand, and began to channel my thoughts down.

My assistant, Dawn, who lost her husband within days of my own husband's passing, called me that Friday afternoon while typing a section of *Sacred Grief,* telling me how it hit home for her. Her husband of twelve years, a Vietnam Veteran, had many a night shared with her the horrors, guilt, and general anxiety that permanently resided in his psyche from war combat. While talking with her, I realized that *Sacred Grief* didn't really address a soldier's grief, usually a male issue. I thanked her for giving me a great detail to the idea of male grief to round off my book.

My brain began to formulate the concept when I realized that I didn't know any veterans personally to understand where the healing needs would center from. The whole idea of war is so antagonistic to my being that I wondered if I could even face the issue to write about it.

Gail, a Doctor of Acupuncture, and I had dinner that Friday night. Gail and I met two years ago. She visits my home state once every three months to treat patients so we have a standing dinner date for the Friday nights she is in town.

During our dining experience, out of the clear blue sky and without any prompting from me, she related the story of helping a Vietnam Veteran's blind daughter regain her sight through homeopathic medicine in her home state. As a result of this success, the vet persuaded her to go to Texas, his home state, where she treated a group of forty-two other Vietnam Veterans for various physical and emotional diseases once weekly every three months for five years with great success. To heal them, especially on an emotional level, where most disease resides, she had become intimate with the concept of survivor's guilt, a part of soldiering that cuts deep into surviving combat veterans. Imagine God providing me a well-qualified guide to my quest to understand the grief of veterans. We discussed her take on survivor's guilt at great length.

God had provided the spark of an idea in the morning, and by eleven o'clock that evening when Dr. Gail left my home, I had received everything I needed to understand and complete the section on soldier grief. Simple yet complicated details designed to help me achieve a life path mission.

These particularly designed details also came at a time where, as a writer, I internally needed confirmation of my path as a writer of a grief manual. God's details are like the Energizer bunny; they keep giving, and giving and giving! Are you open to receiving them? Are you giving thanks for them? Gratitude for God's details will certainly ensure they keep on coming, coming, and coming.

Chapter 5

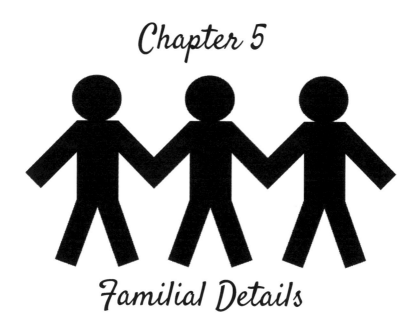

Familial Details

FOR YEARS, KEN'S COMPANY AUTHORIZED THE WEARING OF JEANS ON Fridays. The cost of the privilege was two dollars each week. Then, every year at Christmas, needy families would be gifted with clothes and toys using the jeans money for this purpose. This year, Ken was asked if he could deliver the wrapped packages for seven different families to the church who organized the families in need.

On that same day, Ken was sitting at his ninety-two-year-old mother's table having lunch when out of the clear blue she began to tell him about the worst Christmas she had ever had. It was a time when her five kids were still young. Her husband Ernest was fired from his job for drinking while at work, and they had no money to buy any gifts for the kids. She further related to Ken that, thankfully, some church in the neighborhood caught wind of the situation and provided gifts for each of the kids, so no one was the wiser.

Mary, the woman at the church who coordinated this year's families receiving the gifts, asked Ken if he could help her deliver the gifts directly to one of the families. It was the Jones family to be exact. A single mom with five boys.

When they pulled up to the house, Ken was a little taken aback. Three very large African American boys were looming on the porch. He was sure this was why Mary asked him to help her deliver just this one bag of gifts as he himself was intimidated by the porch "gang." However, Mary wasn't intimidated at all and explained that one of the boys was the Jones family's fourteen-year-old named Ernest. Ken had a grandson who was fourteen years old. Ernest was as tall as Ken, six foot one, so when in the house, Ken looked him straight in the eyes as he talked with him about basketball, school, and ultimately his college plans. Ken saw Ernest was any typical fourteen-year-old kid.

Upon departing, Mary mentioned to Ken that she should have included Ernest when she was passing out children's needs. Apparently, Ernest's mother did not ask for help for her fourteen-year-old son. Ernest expressed that he was just glad his younger four brothers would have some gifts under the tree.

On the way back to the church to drop Mary off, Ken stopped at a sports store and purchased a gift card from Santa and asked Mary if she could be sure it got into Ernest's hand for Christmas. Later, Ken was amazed after thinking about all of the details of the day. How could it be that seventy some years later he was able to provide for an Ernest what an Ernest could not provide for him? Ken never knew a church was responsible for the gifts they received that Christmas past.

Later that night he called his Mom and tearfully related his joy-filled story to her. Mom could finally see, seventy years later, a purpose for the worst Christmas she ever had. Mom passed before the next Christmas came, however, Ken knew that she left understanding that things aren't always as they seem. That what may have appeared as the worst Christmas she ever had, seventy years later brought light and meaning, the real purpose of Christmas, to her son and a young man named Ernest.

Family history and experiences are God designed, as God uses every relationship to set foundations for light to be channeled for the collective. These other familial details should help further this understanding.

Purposeful Accident

George, a forty-two-year-old manager of a big box retail store, slipped in the shower one October and his entire life changed. Recently married to Mona, an employee at his store that he left his wife of twenty-five years for, they had just celebrated the first birthday of their new daughter, Theresa. George became incapacitated for six months, unable to even have physical therapy until his bone mended with the assistance of two titanium rods surgically installed.

Needless to say, George's life was a hot mess. His company let him go because he was unable to work. His two grown daughters were not speaking to him because they were still mad over how he left their mother. He had no income, no health insurance, and no idea of when he would heal. Additionally, he had a wife who culturally would typically never work with a baby in the house and oh, did I mention another baby on the way!

After ten months, all of their savings had been spent, and the only time George had been out of the house was for trips to doctors and hospitals. Please enjoy all of the wonderful "trickle down" experiences that followed for George, Mona, and those closest to them.

George's grown daughters were reunited with their Dad from the first surgery on. They came to love and respect Mona and how she loved and cared for their father. They healed over the pain of their parents' divorce. Even more importantly, they became an essential part of their new half-sister's life, something they may have missed without the healing and forgiveness that took place during their Dad's long recovery.

Mona, after the birth of the second baby, went to work part-time. Unheard of in her culture! She loves her job. She would never have been able to do this without being shamed except her family had no money, and she had no choice.

George, finally able to get around on a walker, began to develop a deep bond with both of his new, young daughters as he was their primary caregiver while Mona was at work. George had always regretted not being part of the process of the raising of his first two daughters due to the long work hours required in the retail business.

Deeper bonding also occurred with George's two older daughters as they took turns spending the time to help their Dad with the two babies while Mona was working.

George's sister Joan benefitted as well. Joan's son and his family were transferred because of his job to another state about six months before George's accident. She had become a vital part of her grandsons' lives before they moved away and deeply felt their absence. She too filled in with the little girls while Mona was working. Her grandmotherly instincts were sated, and she experienced a much deeper love for her brother as a result of all the quiet time they spent together.

Lastly, and probably most importantly, George after seven months of not working found a job outside of the retail world that he loves. He had always disliked the retail business but like a lot of people, had a family to support, so he did what he had to do. George was finally doing something he had a passion for.

Will it take an accident for you to mend the broken parts of your life? We are designed to be loving parents and spouses—to give our talents to our passion while on planet Earth. Why wait for trauma to set us on the right path? Everything we need is or will be provided.

Credit Cards

Barbara Jane tells this story: She and her husband Ken have been married ten years, and recently had a huge disagreement over a home remodeling project. The conflict festered over two weeks when finally their inability to compromise resulted in a full-scale volcanic eruption. They began sleeping in separate bedrooms, a rarity for them, as part of their premarital template strictly prohibited them from going to bed angry.

Barbara Jane stated that this was the final straw for her in this relationship and felt that divorce was most likely inevitable. Fortunately, the remodeling issue was resolved. The entire next day, however, Barbara Jane heard her mind tell her the marriage was over, and further that she should start preparing for a divorce as she was growing tired of the discordance between their two "type A" personalities. As it happened, Barbara Jane stopped to fill her gas tank the next morning only to discover her company credit card was declined for use.

That evening, Barbara Jane and her husband had plans to attend an event starring one of their grandchildren. Barbara Jane had decided to meet Ken there as she was sure she could not stand the sight of him for the moment. Before she knew it, at 4 p.m., she found herself in her favorite food store picking up a pre-made dinner for her and Ken before attending the play. At the checkout counter, her family Visa card was declined. She was just sure that Ken, in anticipation of a pending divorce, had already begun the separation process by removing her name from their credit cards.

With a sense of ferocity, she dialed Ken. His tone was much different than the night before which caused Barbara Jane to take a deep breath and chill a little. She gently confronted him about the Visa card and wondered why hers didn't work. Ken had used his card that day, and it worked fine. He offered to call the bank to find out what the problem was. He had used it because his company gas credit card, like hers, was declined that morning. So all day he thought Barbara Jane had had him removed from the company credit card just like she thought he had removed her from the family credit card. The truth was, the company gas credit card was merely over the limit, a theft prevention tool Barbara Jane had installed years ago.

Ken had all day to see and feel what a divorce might look like to him from his gas credit card not working in the morning. Thinking he was removed from the company's gas privileges did not sit well with him. God used the quirks of the credit cards to show them both what it might feel like to not be together anymore.

Barbara Jane didn't like the prospect of divorce either. As it turned out, the family credit card that Barbara Jane was using was an old credit card. She was not using the newly issued one they had just received, which is why hers didn't work in the grocery store. God, using two different credit cards under two different circumstances to remind two great people of their value to each other. By the way, the remodeling project that sparked this event was, within the next three days, finally agreed upon and eventually finished.

Oh, the paths we sometimes take to get to the next step! How does God manage all these details?

Chapter 6

Critter Details

ONE OF THE LEADING ANIMAL TOTEM MYSTICS IS TED ANDREWS, WHO explains that animals are guides for our "soul path." He teaches one to be aware of the animals, insects, birds, and reptiles that call to us or who repeatedly appear in our life since this is a "natural" way to receive communication from a source greater than ourselves.

Being in "critter tune" can provide life-changing guidance. These narratives are good examples of what can happen when one pays attention to the wonders of God's details through nature. For me, two "totems" have always been pervasive in my life: the heron and the spider. These appearances have not always been pleasant experiences either.

As a wee child, perhaps five, I remember bringing a dead bird in from the outdoors as a gift for my mother. A very "cat-like" gift. Not so ironic, as my name is Catherine and my initials as a child were C A T. She was changing the sheets on a bed when I caught her off guard with the bird in my hand. She saw me and screamed in fright. I, in turn, ran in the other direction through a glass door (this was before glass-safety requirements) and as a result, I became petrified of birds. I mean *petrified* until I was twenty-seven years old. Then one day, someone brought me a bird in a cage to care for while they moved out of state. It was then that I decided enough was enough, and I used that bird to work through my "fear" of birds.

Within a few years of that healing experience, birds were nesting all over my yard, and their messages were a "healing" balm to me on many other issues needing resolution. It was then that the heron first appeared to me and it has been in my space ever since. The message of the heron was that security and stability are defined differently for me. This knowledge has helped me to understand early on that my life path will not be well ordered and typical. I have learned that others will look at me and sometimes roll their eyeballs. It is something I must accept. The fact that I'm wired uniquely, the message of the heron, was a huge relief to understand in my young adult years.

Critters will bring you God's details even if you aren't conscious of what they might be carrying. Personal adventures can be so much more uplifting and long-lasting if you are aware and in tune with them.

Perhaps the following "critter detail" stories will help you along your own path of discovery

Then Came the Duck

Panda Dog, as we had affectionately called her, had come to us from Bill's mom. After having Panda for twelve years, Mom decided to move into a condominium where no dogs were allowed, let alone German Shepherds. My future husband talked about his love for German Shepherds since our first date. We were working on our wedding planned for three months away when the "adoption" call came in. Never being a pet owner before, I certainly wasn't excited about taking on a big dog.

Panda proved to be a sweetheart. Well-mannered and considerate, it took all of three minutes to fall in love with her. Stubborn in her own way, she was a terrific example of the unconditional love dogs are famous for teaching. We found ourselves planning outings that included Panda Dog. It seemed as though if Panda didn't go, we didn't go. Bill even had a sun cover custom made to protect Panda during our boat outings. Panda's presence had an effect on Bill. Childless himself, he started to act like a doting father. She seemed to open his heart in a way I had never seen. Panda was thirteen years old the following May which was relatively old for a German Shepard dog. We were thankful she was so healthy. Bill, a chiropractor, gave her vitamins for her hips and installed a water purifier in our home to ensure our baby put only the purest liquids in her body.

Because I fed her, I think I was her favorite. One thing for sure, when Bill and I ever fought, it was uncanny how Panda would sit at the foot of the person who was "right" in the argument. Somewhere between Panda's fourteenth and fifteenth birthday the inevitable happened. Panda couldn't walk anymore. Deciding what to do when your pet's health is declining was something Bill just refused to face. Never assuming Panda could be in pain, we used a large towel to carry her outside twice a day. She had a plush doggie pillow she perched on while looking out a door wall to beautiful scenery. Her appetite was still healthy.

About two months after Panda's incapacities began, one of Bill's patients, knowing we lived on the water, brought in a baby duck that he rescued from some kids for five dollars. Bill agreed to see the baby duck to adulthood.

So in my husband's natural healing way, he built a small house out of a cardboard box with doors and windows for "Quackers" to sleep inside. We all took turns cuddling it and hand-feeding it. Bill purchased food specifically for ducks. Panda and Quackers would sun themselves together. Quackers would sit right next to Panda—as if Panda was her mother. Ten days after Quackers arrived, Panda had a seizure and went to doggie heaven. My husband was devastated beyond words. He never lost anyone he loved as much as our Panda Dog. Death was a new experience for which he was unprepared to handle.

My grandmother used to say that God never gives you a problem without also giving you the way to solve that problem. Well, thank you God for that duck! Bill's regular daily routine had called for Panda to get morning and evening care. Quackers, who was even more demanding, required a lot of attention. He built a cage for her as she grew. He was entirely focused on caring for Quackers. She was with us for five more months before she decided it was time to be a wild duck. She came to help my husband through his grieving process. I guess you could call it a duck detail.

Deer

I had diligently prepared for five months for a seminar I was producing and speaking at about converting your IRA into self-directed real estate investments.

The big day had finally arrived, and I went home to change my clothes and pick up my husband who had agreed to attend. When I pulled in the driveway, I was upset to see my husband cutting the grass on his lawn tractor. Clearly, he was not ready to go. When I confronted him, he informed me he wasn't coming. I was shocked, hurt, and naturally upset. I knew to have a successful seminar I needed to be calm, but I wasn't sure if I could recover in time to be completely focused on my talk.

I went into the house and looked out the front window. A full-grown doe had swum across the river and landed in our yard. I had lived in this house for fifteen years and had never seen a deer in our yard.

After consulting my animal message research books, I learned that the deer message was to "adapt" to my circumstances as deer have an uncanny ability to adapt to whatever habitat they are faced with. They bring us the opportunity to express a gentle love which in my case was the move to immediately forgive my husband for abandoning me as I felt I needed his presence for the success of my seminar. I needed to adapt.

The deer's presence, or should I say the details of the doe appearing in perfect timing was a reminder to me to adapt to what I could not change. That God detail kept me on track through the entire event. It was a huge success.

Nuthatch

One spring, the noise from a new nesting brood of birds in our massive Grandfather willow tree (a high nasal yank-yank-yank sound) was somewhat irritating as it never seemed to stop. Passerby's even made comments and inquired about the new din adding drama to the neighborhood. I couldn't seem to get a peek at this new avian who had invaded my own peaceful brood with her noisy nest of squeaking babies. This added to my curiosity.

Eventually, the baby birds must have become sated or able to feed themselves because the yank-yank-yanking sound stopped. In late October, preparing my garden for winter's blast, I finally caught sight of my newest tenant—a red-breasted nuthatch.

Like the mating swans whose nest my yard has hosted for the last fifteen years, I was curious as to what message Mother Nature was sending me with the nuthatches. This led me to an excellent resource on this subject, *Animal Speak* by Ted Andrews.

It seems the nuthatch comes into our lives to teach us that we must learn the importance of acknowledging and then blending the spiritual, material, and or physical aspects of our lives in everything we do. The nuthatch travels from the top of trees downward, head first, with the "upper" equating to the spiritual and "lower" to the material essence of things. The flight downward is unusual bird behavior. Andrews mentions in his definitions of the spiritual powers of the nuthatch that for further information one should visit the "Hanged Man" card in a deck of Tarot cards. A friend gave me a beautifully crafted deck of Tarot cards which I've never really used. So, off I went to dig these cards up.

Seems the Hanged Man card, number twelve in the deck, shows a man hanging upside down by one foot holding on to a dragonfly, a show of faith by the hanged man. Faith is defined as the ability to surrender to a higher (spiritual) force. One interpretation of the Hanged Man card says new perspectives (usually a change of mind) are required to move forward.

This message came at a time where I was considering transitioning from a sales career to dedicating myself to writing and teaching—inner passions I have basically ignored for all my sixty years.

Further interpretation of The Hanged Man card directed me to a yoga pose called the Bow. Lying face down, you grasp your ankles behind yourself and slowly raise your legs and trunk at the same time as high as possible, holding for fifteen seconds. The Bow is designed to open your chest to a flow of energy that can direct new focus to the mind—the place where decisions are made.

I was genuinely amazed at how different and free I felt after doing this yoga exercise for fifteen seconds every morning and every night for a week. I literally felt free of stress. More importantly, I was open to receive new ideas for writing and getting more out of life. All because of a little nest of irritating squeaky birds who appeared late summer one year in my yard.

What's irritating to you that may lead you to dig a little deeper? After all, a beautiful pearl starts as an "irritation" in the clam before its beauty can be expressed. Imagine the power you could have in your life if you could see irritation as a detail for change in your life.

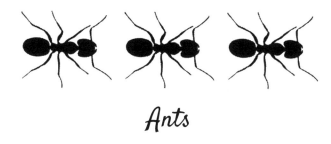

Ants

Nothing in life is free. Here's how I learned that with the help of God's details. I was one of a three-person partnership whose purpose it was to buy, rehab, and sell houses. One of our projects required that a large tree be removed from one of our properties, as the tree was rotted and prospectively going to fall and damage the roof.

Between the three of us, I was assigned the task of obtaining bids and disposing of the tree. Now all three of us had fireplaces in our homes, but in my greed, I negotiated that ALL the wood from the ill-fated tree was to be delivered to my house.

Within a week of the wood delivery, I started to see carpenter ants in my house. Come to find out, the tree that we took down contained a carpenter ant infestation. Although carpenter ants prefer to establish their habitat inside moist wooden hollow areas (such as dead trees), the inside of my house was clearly in the way of their hunt.

I had to have the house exterminated twice to get rid of those giant black critters. It ended up being the exact cost that a cord of non-ant infested wood would have been. Oh, if I had just bought a cord of wood instead of greedily ignoring my partners' rights to any benefits redeemed from our holdings.

God detailed the cost of my greed perfectly. It was a clear lesson that nothing in life is free and a God detail I have fallen back on as a reminder of the result of greed many times over and over in my life.

Ant infestation a God detail? Absolutely! Can you look back at an infestation (insects, people, germs, disease, etc.) you experienced and see God's hands in it?

Praying Mantis

A commercial property that I structured a transaction on had the prospective tenant renting the building for a year before he would close it as a purchase. The tenant paid all his rent up front for a year as an inducement to rent, rather than buy, which was the owner's preference. On the first anniversary date of the lease, after talking with all parties, I scheduled a sales closing, excited to finally receive payment for my services rendered a year ago. The closing was canceled as the seller could not provide clear title to the purchaser. Two weeks later another closing was scheduled. This time it was the buyer who called and indicated his "money man" was out of town. He didn't have the money to close until his money man returned from extended European travel. The original lease provided for a six-month extension with tenant paying rent monthly. We waited for the "money man" to reappear.

The tenant/buyer didn't pay his monthly rent as was required by the six-month lease extension. The owner then had his attorney file documents to begin eviction of the tenant/buyer. This action sparked the buyer to obtain his funds to close. The buyer's attorney called me, and I started the process of gathering updated documents and closing papers to finalize a closing. The closing was scheduled to take place the following Friday at 2:00 p.m. at the title company's office. Even if you can't grasp all of the above details, I'm sure you won't have any problem understanding God's hand in what followed.

Two weeks before the call from the buyer to "reschedule" the closing, I was out of town but still conducting business. Before I left, I had previously talked with a real estate attorney I had never met. I saw his name tied to a class action suit and out of curiosity called for details. I was impressed with him. Good real estate attorneys are tough to find, so I jotted his name in my traveling steno pad. I highlighted his name in lime green so I would remember to transfer this man's name and phone number on to something important when I returned home for future reference.

The Wednesday before the scheduled Friday closing, I noticed a praying mantis sitting by the screen door on my porch. He perched in one spot all afternoon and then at around 5:00 p.m. moved to the screen door until it was dark, when he finally vanished. I've visited this location for ten years and for long periods. I never saw a praying mantis anywhere in the area.

Thursday arrived, and the seller sent me a very nasty text indicating he was not going to pay my commission, so he wasn't going to come to the closing. Legally, the original contract was airtight as to my fee, so I knew he had to pay me. However, the closing could not take place if he didn't come. The remedy would be for everyone to sue everyone and force a closing which is costly and more important, timely.

On a Wednesday night prior, the buyer told me in confidence that he had someone walk in his door and offer him twice the amount he was going to pay the current owner to sell it to him. He was very excited at the opportunity to make such a quick profit. Also on Thursday, the seller let the buyer know that he wasn't coming to the closing because he didn't want to pay me. Of course, the buyer panicked because he had this verbal commitment to double his money in one week. We were talking hundreds of thousands of dollars. He called me and offered to pay just half of my commission out of his pocket to get me to assuage the seller. However, I never discount my brokerage fees and was certainly not going to do so on a transaction I put so much time into and waited so long for. Additionally, it was extremely insulting and hurtful to be denied what I was owed which caused me to dig my heels in on this issue. I went to bed Thursday night tossing and turning over this issue.

The dilemma to me was: do I take the Zen road of "no resistance," a path I find offers the most internal peace but not always the most material peace, or do I fight to the end to preserve what I had already earned? I finally fell asleep well past midnight.

At 2 a.m., I awoke with a start, and a vision of that praying mantis popped in my head. I have learned that birds, animals, and insects can bring messages of love, strength, courage, ideas, etc. to help our life along. I had wanted to see what the message of the praying mantis was since it appeared. So, while still in bed I googled "praying mantis." I read that the praying mantis comes to us when we've flooded ourselves with so much business activity and chaos, that we can no longer hear our still small voice, the Soul part of us. Further, out of sixteen additional word associations for the praying mantis, four jumped out at me: meditation, empowerment, silence, and direction.

So, at 2:30 a.m., I closed my eyes and began to meditate in the silence, looking for the direction of empowerment. Michigan real estate laws started bouncing around in my head. It felt like I needed to take action and not just walk away and let someone cheat me.

In Michigan, a commercial real estate broker can file a claim/lien against a commercial property for commissions without a court hearing. The closer can escrow up to three times the value of the commission until the dispute can be adjudicated.

In my meditation, all sorts of roadblocks popped up, not the least of which was that if I was going to file a claim, it had to be done before the 2 p.m. scheduled closing that day. I didn't know any good real estate attorneys, my secretary was off on Friday, oh and did I say that I was in Florida and the property sale was in Michigan? On top of all that, I had committed to taking our Florida house guest to the airport for his 3:00 p.m. return flight. Additionally, the form of lien needed, a Lis Pendens, requires an original signature on it for recording, and it must be signed in blue ink, and I wasn't in town. It felt more like worrying than meditation to me.

As I quieted myself taking deep breathes and clearing my mind, a most amazing message came to me. Just two weeks ago I had highlighted in my steno pad, in "praying mantis" green, an excellent real estate attorney's name. That was it! I decided I would call him after 9:00 a.m. If he and I could pull off everything needed before 2:00 p.m., then that's what I would do. And if not, well then that was a sign of letting it go and see how the universe would put it together—one way or the other. I resumed a peaceful sleep.

In route to the airport by 9:00 a.m., I left a message for Mark, the real estate attorney, to call me. I wasn't even sure he would remember me. He returned my call at 9:55 a.m., and I explained what I needed. He could do it, but I needed to get him a copy of the lease where it showed my claim. We were driving on U.S. 1 in the Florida Keys South. Although I had the lease with me in the car, there was absolutely nothing around where I could stop and fax or scan the document—no restaurants, no hotels, no real estate offices. That's when my house guest mentioned that he had just purchased an app that can scan and send documents from his phone. We pulled over and worked from the back of our SUV to scan the seven-page lease to send off to the attorney.

The next hurdle was that the document required my signature in blue ink only for recording. The office had my signature stamp, but it was in black ink. Plus, I had to track my secretary down on her day off and hope she wasn't committed to something else.

Ginger was at the gym when I called her. She had twenty more minutes left to her routine, but she said she could finish and get to the office in forty minutes. I asked her to pick up some blue ink for the signature stamp at the office supply store on her way in. This would mean that Ginger would be at her desk around 11:00 a.m. Still three hours to go. No sweat. The attorney sent the Lis Pendens he prepared to me by 11:30 a.m. While still transporting our house guest, I reviewed the document and sent it to Ginger for my signature, or so I thought. The document is probably still somewhere in the cyber world of loose material since she never received it. Thankfully, I called Ginger at noon to be sure she had stamped my name and recorded it when she advised she hadn't received it. Eek! She also told me there was no blue ink at the office supply store (eek again) but indicated she thought she could manipulate my signature on the document using the computer. I resent the Lis Pendens at 12:45 p.m. Ginger and another office lady were still trying to manipulate and apply the blue ink signature.

I knew that God's hand was in all of this because of the visit by the praying mantis, my highlighting the attorney's name in praying mantis green, and because I woke up at 2 a.m. to receive the message of the mantis. So I was remarkably calm as my husband and I enjoyed lunch at a Key West outdoor restaurant with our house guest. I will admit however, I began to get nervous when I called Ginger at 1:25 p.m. and they still hadn't mastered the signature problem. However, she texted me at 1:30 p.m. that she was on her way to record the Lis Pendens at the courthouse which was directly across the street from the office. I requested she text me when done because I had to notify the closer at the title company of the recorded lien before 2:00 p.m., the scheduled closing time.

At 1:37 p.m., I had still not heard from Ginger. I called her, and she related the following to me: she went up to the recording window at the courthouse where she was told that they don't record these types of liens. However, God had his hands in this and put an attorney in line right behind Ginger, who stepped up to the window and told her they certainly do and to get a supervisor, which she did. The supervisor took the document to record. Ginger had to wait for a copy to send to the title company as proof of the lien. It took ten minutes for the counter help to come back and inform Ginger that they don't accept documents notarized by relatives. Ginger's last name is the same as mine, but we are not related. They finally recorded the document at 1:53 p.m. I called the title closer and informed them of the lien. They told the purchaser that they couldn't close unless I receive payment, as I had filed a claim for my commission. The seller had not appeared at the closing as he indicated he wouldn't. However, if and when he sold the property, I (or my estate) would receive my due because of the commission lien on the property.

As it turned out, the buyer who was anxiously awaiting the prospect of doubling his money, went to his bank and brought a check back for my entire commission. They closed the buyer. The seller appeared separately at the close of business that day and finalized the purchase.

In the message of the most beautiful praying mantis, I meditated to connect to source, received empowerment, and directions on every needed step and in my silence (that is, not to argue or dispute over the issue with buyer or seller) received what must have been mine or I would have never received it.

How did my house guest happen to have purchased a scan program before he came to visit? How was it that a real estate attorney was in line behind my secretary at the recording counter? How was it that a praying mantis brought me the messages of empowerment and meditation as well as the color of it as the highlight color of the perfect real estate attorney in my steno pad? Right is right. In this case, God's details confirmed it.

Animal Medicine

Eight months after my husband died suddenly of a heart attack, I met Howard. I was hardly interested in the dating scene, but Howard was gentle, patient, and aware of my vulnerability. He took great strides in protecting that vulnerability, and within five months I had come to care deeply for him.

Although a wonderful man, Howard had a large family, a demanding job, church activities he loved, and male friendships that he had developed over the last seven years of his single life that took most of his attention. Howard professed his love for me many times. Howard would call me every Sunday evening to work out what days he could "slot me in" his very busy schedule.

Still fairly guarded, we had moved into sharing some delightful, intimate (non-sexual) times together. After an exceptionally deep and moving Thursday evening together, I felt that we had reached a new level of intimacy but became disappointed and disillusioned by his lack of any phone calls following these dates. He was heading up north with the guys for the weekend and while away, I received an animal message that changed the course of our relationship.

On three previous occasions, we had had serious heart to heart talks where I expressed my need for emotional intimacy. Howard always agreed with me and apologized for his aloofness with his emotions. He would always apologize and ask me to be patient, so he could learn how to be more intimate.

It soon became apparent to me that Howard was never going to have enough time for me. All those "other" activities he put before us I quickly learned were about intimacy avoidance for him. I knew that for our relationship to go any further, I needed to be cherished and honored as the most important person in his life.

Every emotion I could experience was reeling on my Soul while Howard was away for the weekend. I prayed for the wisdom to guide me to my highest truth in our relationship.

Saturday night, while on my way home from dinner I was awed to discover a wolf standing about thirty feet from the edge of the road near the exit from the restaurant driveway. I had lived in this neighborhood for twenty-four years and never saw a wolf before. I immediately went to my studio and found my copy of *Animal Speak*, by Ted Andrews, an excellent dissertation on animal totems. I was amazed to read about and interpret what the presence of the wolf had meant. It was a message telling me that I needed to honor my feminine needs. If Howard was unable to be part of that, then I needed to move on.

On my way to Church the next morning, Howard called, and I told him that I was unable to see him any longer since he wasn't able to give me what I needed. With his usual class and style, he convinced me to agree to a five-week hiatus. I was emotionally distraught as I had grown to care intensely for Howard.

Later that Sunday afternoon I attended a seminar for Sunday School teachers. The facilitator had provided information on the nine ways people learn. She then directed us to select one of the nine tables set up for round table discussions, which were moderated and designed to give us new ideas as to how people learn. The goal was to sit with like-minded learners and work through an exercise to help us better teach our students. My group was about learning through nature. After a few minutes, I told the three other people at my table about my recent wolf experience and at their request added my interpretation of the wolf sighting.

Two amazingly detailed things happened! One of the men at the table, Sparky, informed us that his father was a Shaman. A Shaman is defined as an intermediary between the natural and supernatural worlds. He asked me a few questions about the wolf and then gave me his interpretation of the wolf appearing in my life. He said, "In the Native American tradition, the belief is that it is our journey to travel the 'red road.'" Sparky described the red road as the high road, the road that leads to our highest truth and integrity. He further stated that illness (disease) comes when we veer off the high road even just a little. In yoga terms, that would be like moving away from your center. "Leaning a little" to a Native American means that as you lean away from the road, a little of your truth or energy leaks out, and you are not equipped to experience the good life our birthright offers fully.

Sparky continued with, "The first rule of the Native American tradition is that the Divine Feminine must be protected at all costs."

This statement was a clear message to me that I was wise to remove myself from any relationship that did not honor and protect my Divine Feminine. The wolf, standing by the side of the road was telling me to stay on the "red road" of my truth. The wolf was encouraging me to make choices that my heart did not want to make; do not veer off the path or I will lose my center.

Then, the only other lady at the table, a zookeeper, put a book in front of me that she had just purchased that day called *All My Relations: Living with Animals as Teachers and Healers.* The animal depicted on the cover? A wolf.

I knew at once that I had made a good choice for myself to move on from Howard, even though it was hard and a little self-centered. That lovely woman gifted me the book, and to this day, years later, I still open the wolf book when I need reminding to stand in my truth.

How is it that a rare wolf sighting occurs on a Saturday night, the next day I sit at a round table with the son of a Shaman and a zookeeper who just happened to buy a book on wolves, and then gifted me the book at the time I was seeking translation on the wolf message?

God's Details? Beyond amazing.

Chapter 7

Details from Beyond

BEVERLY, A WIDOW FROM FLORIDA, MARRIED ALMOST FIFTY YEARS, TELLS the story of receiving a message from her husband five months after he died suddenly of a heart attack at seventy-eight years of age.

It was a beautiful sunny day, and Beverly went on her deck to enjoy the golf course view. Sitting on the deck, was a semi-deflated helium balloon that said, "Just Because." She lifted it to see if the wind would take it away, but it was too deflated to be lifted away. Beverly tied a couple of loops of the hanging string on the balloon around her lounge chair and retired for the evening.

In the morning, Beverly found the "Just Because" Balloon in the center of the glass atrium of her home. That meant that this deflated balloon untied itself and lifted over the roof and settled in the atrium.

Beverly's husband was always doing nice things for her . . . "just because."

Not all of God's details are earth shattering or life changing. But they are all light filled. God uses messages from the beyond to bring comfort, direction, and sometimes even understanding of where we are all eventually headed. After you read some of these stories, take a moment to think about your own experiences from beyond the living.

Dead People Messages

Jill's mother was always known to be connected psychically to dead people. She told Jill many times that she would send butterflies and hummingbirds to her after she passed as a sign and reminder that she was with her and still loved her.

Fifteen years after her mother passed, for the entire month of August, Jill had many, many visits from monarch butterflies as well as an abundance of hummingbirds who made their appearance.

One August day, Jill casually mentioned to Mary, her boss of seven years, details of her insect and hummingbird visits and related her mom's pre-death message. Mary was flabbergasted! She, too, had noticed a lot of hummingbirds cross her path during August as well, and it seemed like one monarch butterfly was hanging around her no matter where she went. Mary even received two hummingbird feeders for her 70th birthday that same month. What was so amazing to Mary was that she had been receiving messages from "a small still voice" about making plans for who would be her future caregiver when necessary as she had no family she could rely upon. Somewhere in that month of August, before their chance discussion, Mary heard that small still voice say, "Ask Jill to be your health and elder care advocate."

After Jill finished telling Mary the story of her mom and butterflies and hummingbirds, Mary knew those same critters were sending her confirmation of that still small voice she heard urging her to ask Jill to be her old-age caregiver. Mary immediately said to Jill, "I have no family, and you have no mother. Will you make sure I'm cared for if unable to do so myself?" Jill, with tears streaming down her face, was ecstatic to be chosen to see Mary through to the end of her life as needed. The message of Jill's mother, a significant God detail, brought two people's needs together in a beautiful way.

In the Nick of Time

This is a true story from an article written twenty years ago in a local newspaper and confirmed by this writer. Although this "God detail" saga is common, I almost didn't add it to the collection. However, what struck me was how Joe was guided to choose winning numbers, where the lottery ticket was hidden for a year, and the God details in the timing that made Esther and Joe comfortably rich for the duration of their lives.

In January of 2005, Joe had a dream wherein his deceased parents appeared and encouraged him to purchase a lottery ticket. A regular player and always using the same numbers, Joe had a feeling from the dream and decided to change the numbers and used a combination of each of their birth dates when he purchased his next lottery ticket. At that time, he was wearing a new jacket his wife had recently bought for him, and Joe absentmindedly put the ticket in his jacket pocket.

Joe didn't exactly care for the new jacket, so when he took it off for the day, he put it in the back of his coat closet and never gave it or the lottery ticket another thought.

Move forward 362 days to Friday, January 6, 2006. Joe's wife, Esther, had recently purchased another new coat for Joe that she noticed he wasn't wearing. When asked by Esther why he wasn't wearing it, he commented that he didn't like it. Esther asked Joe to pull it out of the closet so she could return it, claiming they "didn't need to have a closet full of coats he didn't like." Something about that remark, for some reason, caused Joe to don last year's leather jacket that he had only worn once, where of course, he discovered the old lottery ticket.

Out of curiosity more than anything else, Joe checked the numbers online and saw that the ticket matched all of the numbers. He knew he had won something but wasn't sure what.

That same night, the local evening news reported that the pay-off on a 1.5 million dollar ticket containing the numbers on Joe's ticket was going to expire Monday. That following Monday morning, Joe and Esther made their way to the lottery collection office just in the nick of time. One day later and the money allotted to pay off Joe's ticket would have defaulted to the state treasury fund.

How do these coincidences happen? From a dream, some numbers. From an unwanted coat found 362 days later, a winning lottery ticket. Any later and Joe and Esther's life would have been different. God's details, at work in the nick of time even with lottery tickets.

Chapter 8

The Littlest Detail

JAMIE LOST HER HUSBAND, JASON, IN A VIOLENT MANNER TWENTY-ONE years ago. One recent September Wednesday night in a dream, he appeared to her in her garage. After hugging him, she asked him where he was going. He stated, "I'm going with Wes," his younger brother, "to a party."

Since Wes never fully recovered from the loss of his brother, she knew she needed to let Wesley know that his brother appeared to her and mentioned his name. She texted him telling him about her dream. Wesley's response was ecstatic to hear from his brother, especially because it was his birthday. Jason was going to Wes's birthday party in Jamie's dream. Jamie was glad she was used to brighten Wesley's birthday.

God's littlest details are always gently urging us toward the release of a hurtful past not only for ourselves but also for others as in Jamie and Wes's case. Do you see any of God's details at work for the healing of your past?

Birthday Surprises

Suzie celebrated her fiftieth birthday three months after her husband passed from an eight-year battle with cancer. On that day she was looking for something in her husband's closet when a box on the top shelf, way in the rear, caught her eye. After Suzie struggled to get it down, she opened the box and discovered a hundred dollar bill and two fifty dollar bills that she had given her husband for his fiftieth birthday three years earlier. She had fashioned them into the shape of airplanes because his birthday gift was an airplane ride so he could go skydiving. Bob was never well enough to take the skydiving trip. Suzie also found the card she had given him encouraging him to "fly high" in his life.

Suzie knew that the discovery of the card and the dollar bills fashioned into airplanes on her birthday was a God detailed message of healing love from her husband for her birthday.

Dessert

Donna tells the story of her eighty-three-year-old mother who, before her death, made Donna promise that there would be no funeral. She instead requested a memorial service when the family was ready and asked that it be a simple celebration of her life.

Several months after her mother passed they had a celebration dinner. Donna had invited over one hundred people. When selecting the menu, she hadn't paid particular attention in choosing the dessert as the restaurant assured her that their desserts were delicious and not to worry about it.

The dinner was delightful, but it didn't compare to the surprise and glee experienced when the dessert was brought out. One hundred hot fudge cream puffs were served. Donna began to cry because hot fudge cream puffs were her mother's favorite dessert. Donna knew that her mother was safe and pleased with the celebration dinner.

God definitely had his hand in this. One small dessert detail provided the joy for over one hundred people.

Pin Number

Mark and his dad Lyle owned a heating and cooling company together for over five years. When Mark's dad died of a sudden heart attack, Mark was devastated. They were not only business partners but best friends as well.

After getting only three hours of sleep the night Lyle passed, Mark felt he had to go to work and let everyone know what had happened. When he walked into the office, he discovered that the secretary had forgotten to leave the air conditioner on overnight. It felt like it was one hundred degrees in the building. Mark checked the thermostat and in doing so went into an even deeper shock than he was already in from the previous night's event.

The numbers on the thermostat, which should have indicated the current temperature, read 7777. This was Lyle's PIN that he used to access his ATM and computer. Upon seeing that number, Mark felt a wave of warm, fuzzy energy. He knew immediately that his father was okay. That number never left the thermostat. He had to replace the thermostat to get the air conditioning turned on.

Janet and Russ

Janet and Russ were married fifteen years. For their anniversary on July 12, Russ had ordered a gift for Janet by mail. He told her about the purchase without revealing what it was because it was not going to arrive in time for their anniversary. Between the time he ordered it and their anniversary, Russ had a fatal heart attack that took him quickly. Janet was left in a state of shock and had forgotten all about the gift.

Two months after Russ passed, a package arrived for her. Much to Janet's surprise, a tabletop water fountain was in the box. Its design covered in butterflies.

Butterflies were hugely symbolic to Janet. She had always thought butterflies represented the presence of her mother and grandmother who had both passed. Every time she saw a butterfly she was sure it was a visit from one of them.

The same day Janet received the butterfly fountain, Russ's place of business delivered to her a very large toolbox from his work. As the delivery man was unstrapping it from the truck, a big yellow butterfly began dive bombing him as if saying "here I am." The message of butterflies is typically metaphysically related to regeneration and rebirth. Janet felt confident that the influx of all the butterflies in one day was a distinct and clear message from Russ encouraging her to move forward with the next steps of her life.

Chapter 9

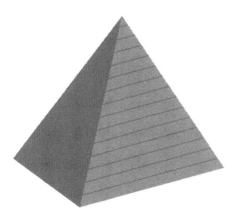

Nature's Details

ALTHOUGH STONE PYRAMIDS WERE NOT MADE BY NATURE, THE SACRED geometry that they contain was. The word pyramid means "fire in the middle" or "fire in the belly."

Pyramids were originally built to protect Egyptian kings since the kings were considered to have been chosen by the gods to serve as mediators between them and people. Egyptians believed that a part of the spirit (Ka) remained within the king's body, so the body needed to be appropriately preserved, or mummified, to house this spirit. The four sides of the pyramid were designed to maintain the essence of the king and help the king's soul ascend and return to the gods. To this day it is still unknown how this design technology was discovered.

It has been written that what man intends for one thing, God uses for something else. Scientists now understand that pyramids are actually amplifiers of various types of electric fields including electromagnetic waves, cosmic (sun) rays, gravitational waves, and the electrical discharges that surround our planet. A pyramid's geometrical design somehow attracts these various forms of energy, mixes them inside the middle third, the belly, to create an amazing three-dimensional globe of harmonic vibration from a generating spin field at the pyramid's highest point. This "combo" energy then emanates from the four corners of the pyramid walls. Scientists tell us this powerful mix of energy is considered a life-giving force. It is not naturally produced anywhere else on Earth which may explain the attraction for millions of people around the world who trek to the famed pyramids.

Built by occult-like Egyptians using slaves looking to preserve a king's body, pyramids have shown science how to combine lower vibrational energy into higher vibrational energy using the sacred geometric structure of the pyramid. Not to mention, as an added benefit, the geometric construction of the pyramid for some reason, does not allow the growth of bacteria responsible for decomposition of the human body. The entropy, that is, the lack of order that bacteria feed on, is almost non-existent due to the intensity of the energy collected in the pyramid. Science has learned much from the study of pyramids. A God detail provided over 4,600 years ago to a group of pagans who supposedly were not aware of the true magnificence of their creation that is helping scientists understand its powerful implications today.

Read on to discover even more fantastic nature details. Proof positive that things take time and when the student appears, so will the teacher.

Palm Trees

One year, at our winter home, a house three streets over had a high-intensity spotlight that shined directly into my eyes through my second story bedroom window. Oh sure, I could have closed the window and the blinds, but I would have had to forego the benefit of the warm ocean breeze in our home—precisely the reason we come to Florida. After a week of dealing with this irritation, I decided to ride over, meet the owner, and ask if he could adjust the light fixture down just a degree or two.

I had just returned from walking to the back of his house where the light was, where I noticed that the hinge on the fixture allowed a downward adjustment. I was fully intent on walking to the front door to talk with the owner, when the security guard, on a regular patrol of our gated community, came at me with flailing arms. "Stop!" was her immediate shout, "What are you doing?" After my explanation, she told me that the man living in the "lighthouse" was a hermit and a rude one at that. She informed me that he has cameras around his house, and it was illegal for me to even go on his property without his permission.

Relating this story to my "knight in shining armor" husband ignited his testosterone defense system. First, he planned to go over there, and if that didn't work, he would go to the office and file a complaint.

Around this same time, I was intensely studying the Bhagavad Gita, the Hindu book of wisdom, which teaches that the path to a happier life is an adherence to the concepts of non-judgment, non-attachment, and non-resistance. I requested of my husband that we unite and give this problem over to God. I said, "Let's see how it will be handled without my resistance and your testosterone."

After three weeks of the light in my eyes, I started noticing that when the wind was blowing a certain way, the palm trees outside my "light-filled window" managed to create a psychedelic pattern that was kind of cool when my eyes were closed. I embraced it as art, and the nightlight less awakened my sleep. It took five weeks, but within that time, three palm trees between our house and the hermit's house managed to grow in a way that completely blocked the light from my evening view.

God is in every detail—no matter how trite. Why not see how the philosophy of non-resistance to an annoyance might lead you down a more peaceful and stress-free life path?

Oxygen

Our planet wasn't always oxygen rich. In fact, Earth's original atmosphere was comprised of noxious methane, carbon monoxide, hydrogen sulfide, and ammonia. Scientists tell us that 3.5 billion years ago a single-celled bacteria known as Cyanobacteria was the predominant form of life on early Earth for more than 2 billion years. Through their photosynthetic metabolization process, that is consuming carbon dioxide and releasing oxygen, the oxygen-rich atmosphere we experience today was created. Further, this bacteria, through its repeated collective recolonization, grew a hard sedimentary platform forming the Earth's crust layer by layer, growing upward toward the life-giving energy of the sun.

We humans live on a planet whose atmosphere was created by bacteria. Our mitochondria, the powerhouse or digestive system of our cells, operate today in the same way as the photosynthetic process of the cyanobacteria, known as endosymbiosis in humans. Are we descendants of bacteria?

Bacteria creating oxygen and Earth's crust.

Two billion years to complete.

All in God's perfect timing and amazing details.

Egg

During the human female menstrual cycle, the female produces one egg that waits in the fallopian tubes to be fertilized. (Twins are produced when on occasion two eggs are produced in one month.) If that egg does not get fertilized it is dispelled from the tubes and dissolves in menses flow.

The female menstrual cycle occurs every twenty-eight days and is a God detail designed so that human life continues to propagate. That same process works in chickens except the production process runs between every twenty-one to twenty-three hours instead of every twenty-eight days. Chickens are not mammals, so there are no menses required for their eggs to produce.

Consider the comparison:

A human egg, the size of any other cell in the human body (basically microscopic) with the thickness of a strand of hair, comes along once every twenty-eight days and has the possibility of producing a human being. The chicken egg, the size well known to all, comes along every twenty-two hours. Do you see God's hand in this most amazing process? How is it that the human egg having the diameter of 100 microns (millionths of a meter) is so small when a three-pound chicken produces an egg the size of, well, a chicken egg? And so frequently! Same process, different outcome. Another mind-boggling example of God in nature's details.

The Amazing Dragonfly

Dragonflies are often associated with magic or the fairy realm probably because they have histories that date back 406 million years, long before dinosaurs walked the face of the earth. Dragonflies, perfectly God detailed in every way, teach us the cyclical transformation from life to death to life again. They hatch in water as water bugs, then later relinquish that way of life when they finally climb out of the water, dry, and become amazing creatures of flight. There are 5,700 different species of dragonflies, each with God's perfect details.

Dragonflies have two huge compound eyes that host 28,000 plus facets (lenses). Compare this to the common housefly, which only has 4,000 facets. The dragonfly's excellent range of vision (360°) allows them to detect other insects, predators, and avoid flight collisions.

The pre-dragonfly water bug molts its skin between nine and seventeen times before adulthood. The final molting takes place out of the water. Within one hour of this last shed, the dragonfly will double in size—its wings are finally full-grown at this point.

The wings of the dragonfly move independently of each other with both frontward and backward capabilities. Dragonflies ride on a vortex of air created by their unique wing action. Their wings can flap at thirty flaps per second and they have been known to fly up to thirty miles per hour. Dragonflies are typically known to migrate more than 1,000 miles. The Globe Skimmer, however, was documented in an 11,000-mile migratory flight between Africa and India. Dragonflies are creatures of the sun as they rely on solar energy for warmth often using their wings as reflectors to send the sun's rays to other parts of their body or as deflectors when it's too warm.

Tasty to birds and other predators, immature dragonflies are no stranger to the food chain on this planet as ninety percent of newly hatched dragonflies never see day four of their life. Amazingly designed, millions of years ago, in perfect detail!

Salamander

Here is a God detail that humans may be able to put to future use: The salamander and its unique regenerative abilities. The salamander is a four-legged vertebrate that can walk and swim underwater. Unlike the scaly, clawed lizard it resembles, this amphibian has smooth skin and no claws at the end of its toes. Also unlike its relative the lizard, the salamander has the capacity to regenerate, that is, regrow its four limbs and tail if any or all of them become severed. The salamander's front legs are designed the same as human arms. A severed salamander limb will reproduce with perfection, over and over if need be, with interlocking bones, muscles, even delicate wrist bones with coordinating fingers that are all mechanically rewired to the proper nerves and blood vessels.

Within the first week of limb loss, the salamander's wound begins to cover itself with skin cells that allow debris (dead cells) from the severed limb to return to the bloodstream, which then ignites the regeneration process. This new epidermis layer thickens over the apex of the stump into a transparent tissue. The combination of many cells underneath the transparent wound covering works to regenerate the severed body part with all of its specific functions. A cone-shaped growth emerges from here and eventually, within forty to fifty days, the limb is built and fully functional.

Science has been studying this amazing regenerative process for hundreds of years with the hopes of applying the mysteries of salamander regeneration to the regeneration of parts of the human body. The salamander process, provided by God for the future health and well-being of mankind.

God's details always in the works ready for mankind when mankind is prepared to receive and process them.

Chapter 10

*To be suspicious and greedy when majesty arrives
is the worst arrogance.
Rumi, 13ᵗʰ century Sufi Poet*

A Final Detail

BESIDES THE AMAZING GOD DETAILS THAT SURROUND US LIKE THE pyramids of 4,000 years ago, or the regeneration of the salamander's limbs and tail, what I would hope you gain from these God detail parables is to view all things that occur in your life as God details—yes, even those things that hurt, take something away from you, or add stress to your life. Learning to alter reactions to loss and stress and accepting the things that you experience, whether you judge them good or bad, can be challenging. A sure-fire method for this desirous consciousness change can be triggered by simple thoughts and acts of constant gratitude for things big and small as they occur in your life, i.e., a front row parking space, a delay that made a difference, the song on the radio that brought a smile to your face or reminded you to call someone.

Acts of gratitude can ignite the emotional/mental learning process of accepting the things you cannot change, changing the things you can and garnering the wisdom to know the difference between the two when they occur. This wisdom is taken from the serenity prayer that is memorized by everyone who enters an AA type program. Taking the time to stop and give thanks for all our circumstances as we are in them, whether mentally or verbally, or both, can ignite the mind's ability to see beyond visible circumstances into the ultimate purpose of why things happen.

Try thanking God for every detail, both what appears good and not good, in your life and watch your mind, your body's health, and your overall well-being resonate with joy.

Gratitude, gratitude, gratitude. God is still in the business of miracle-making in our lives, even if our water isn't turning into wine or we are not able to feed 5,000 people with two fish and five loaves of bread.

A Personal Message from the Author

I didn't know until the second publishing of this book that *God Is in the Details* was actually a prequel to my Sacred Series of Conscious Change manuals. Conscious change, defined as change of mind and/or heart with an intention to make Earth a better place to live because *YOU* moved yourself to a higher plane of thought and action, is only possible when one can comprehend that no matter what we are facing, there is a light-filled purpose in it. Accepting our own role in the spiritual evolution of Earth gives compliment to the teachings of the master prophet Jesus, whose many examples on how to live a life were little more than guidelines for our own conscious change.

To be clear, conscious change is an individual path—often lonely and scary. However, as we see from the stories in *God Is in the Details*, the end result is managed by a higher power. We merely need to take the appropriate steps to "consciously change" the taped messages in our minds that don't help move us towards light-filled experiences.

Light-Filled Experience brings results such as joy, happiness, prosperity, and fulfillment. Thoughts and feelings of guilt, anger, fear, greed, jealousy, resentment, etc., DO NOT allow light-filled experiences to manifest in our lives. A decision for conscious change is a decision to create new boundaries for yourself. My Sacred Series of books,

145

Sacred Grief, Sacred Prosperity, Sacred Space, and *Sacred Relationships* can help one do just that—morph from a physical being in the middle of having a human experience to a physical being having a spiritual experience.

The first book in the Sacred Series is *Sacred Grief.* Anyone who has "worked" through *Sacred Grief* has been amazed at how grief took hold of them and didn't let go, as in the case of the 12-year-old girl who lost her horse thirty-five years ago and was still grieving, to the mother who lost her son in a drowning incident twenty-five years ago. Loss of a job, friend, pet, fortune, etc., all have grief as its core energy. Sadness is a form of separation from our source. If not resolved, sadness will linger and block the fullness of the life we were born to enjoy.

Lack mindedness is curable! *Sacred Prosperity* helps one rise above poverty consciousness. God's details are about an abundance of all kinds. When the Jewish prisoner of war hung his Red Cross bag on the lever that prevented movement of the train, which halted the death of a cattle car full of Jewish prisoners, abundance arrived for each and every person on that train. The flow of abundance is a natural right of citizenship on our planet, but like anything else, it has mechanical rules that must be followed. A workbook and manual for those who want a closer relationship with self and ultimately, Soul, *Sacred Prosperity* is designed to help one reach deep inside themselves and discover the secret to a more prosperous existence.

Sacred Space was written to address the seven deadly sins—shadow energy—that is part of the yin-yang balance of Earth. As one works through *Sacred Space*, you will learn to release issues that were filled with fear, guilt, greed, anger, hatred, jealousy, or resentment that still may be lingering on your mind and heart. The energy of the seven deadly sins will ALWAYS separate us from our source. Why not develop a way to eliminate those seven deadly "error messages" from your being so that you can be free to experience their opposites: joy, love, happiness, etc. IT IS POSSIBLE, but you have to do the work to move through it. Consider *Sacred Space*, a resource book for do-it-yourself mental health.

Sacred Relationship, a manual and workbook (soon to be published), focuses on the truth of what relationships are on this planet . . . Opportunities to be closer to Soul's wisdom and guidance. Improving your ability to be in a loving, spirit-filled relationship is the end result of *Sacred Relationship*.

All the Sacred Series Manuals are complete with hundreds of affirmations to "reset" the conscious mind with statements of truth (I am the light of the world or I see only light in this situation or God's will is my will) that can change your life. You simply need to create an intention for conscious change and take the next step! The Sacred Series books can help.

Caveat—Don't invest in any of my Sacred books if you do not want to consciously transform your life.

About the Author

Catherine Wilcox is a self-taught conscious change coach and spiritual advisor who opens pathways of communication from Soul to the ego—a 21st century art. She has personally counseled hundreds of people along the path of healing through the process of forgiveness of self and others. It is her belief and experience that until you take the time to interact (guided or otherwise) with the issues that have blocked your peace and happiness, you will be trapped in unproductive and unhappy life experiences that will play over and over again.

A natural-born teacher, writing "soul synchronizing" lesson guides (*Sacred Grief* and *Sacred Prosperity* to name a few) is her lifelong passion. When she is not photographing nature or fishing in the Florida Keys, she enjoys living in a sleepy water community in Michigan where artists of all genres come to relax and rejuvenate in her wise counsel and beautiful gardens.

Catherine is also an avid blogger and posts her thoughts about Conscious Change online each week. You can read her blogs and find out more by visiting www.soulsequening.com, www.healerstore.com, and www.catfishart.shop. To find out more about Catherine's business manuals, visit www.northstarmanuals.com.

Made in the USA
Columbia, SC
16 December 2020

28227062R00091